UNDER WAY

UNDER WAY

The A-Z Guide to Safe and Successful
Seamanship

BILL BEAVIS

Drawings by Alan Roy

LUTTERWORTH PRESS
Richard Smart Publishing

First published 1978

Published by Lutterworth Press
Luke House, Farnham Road, Guildford, Surrey
and Richard Smart Publishing

Copyright © Bill Beavis, 1978

ISBN 0 7188 7015 8

Printed by John G Eccles
Printers Ltd, Inverness

CONTENTS

ACKNOWLEDGMENTS

I should like to acknowledge the help given in the preparation of this book by the Editors and staff of *Yachting Monthly*, *Motor Boat & Yachting* and *Sail*. I should also like to thank Bridon Fibres and Plastics, the makers of *Braidline* ropes, for permission to publish their recommendations for rope sizes. And finally Group Captain E. F. Haylock for his kindness in allowing me to reprint the section on First Aid which has been taken from his book *Water Wisdom*.

ABANDON SHIP

The first inrush of water following severe hull damage and the dramatic rise in the level of water within the narrow confines of the bilge will suggest that sinking is immediate. However, in most cases of foundering small craft take at least five minutes to sink, and usually much more. Keep your head, launch the dinghy, pick off your approximate position from the chart and send out radio distress call or, if appropriate to do so, fire rockets. Gather food, water, clothing and personal effects, put them in polythene bags and stow them in the dinghy. Take also compass, charts, distress signals, torch, seasick tablets etc. (*see* **Panic Bag**). Standby to abandon but only do so when all else seems hopeless.

If forced into the water it is important that you remain with the boat — tied to it if necessary. Even a swamped or capsized vessel is easier to see than a swimmer. Moreover the boat will support you and obviate the need for physical movement. Even in temperate water it is vital that you conserve body heat and this is most successfully done by keeping still and wearing as many clothes as possible.

If you have good reason to believe your distress signal has been received and land is too far off to be reached, then it is important to remain as close to the scene of foundering as possible. This is your rescuer's search area. Stream drouges to reduce lee drift.

A liferaft is the preferred survival vehicle although the ordinary yachts' dinghy should not be discounted and wherever possible taken in tow. The dinghy will be useful for extra stowage space, for exercise, for towing the liferaft to an intended destination, as a working platform for fishing etc and even as a drouge if filled with water. It will need a cover to protect survivors from exposure and probably require additional buoyancy in the form of fenders, fuel cans etc secured under gunwhales and thwarts.

Panic Bag. This should contain a collection of needed items wrapped where necessary in waterproof material and kept handy. It should include: money, passports, ship's papers, additional clothing, first aid kit, torch, distress signals, drinking cup, anti-seasick tablets, fishing gear, knife, tin opener, heaving line, water and food. A spare lifejacket inside will ensure that the bag floats should it need to be jettisoned.

(*See also*: DISTRESS, RESCUE, SURVIVAL).

AGROUND

Going aground: Waste no time. Hull type and circumstance will decide immediate action:

Go about onto other tack, harden mainsail, trim or back jib, crew to leeward. Boat may heel sufficiently to sail or slew off.

Lower sail, send crew forward to trim boat by the head, reverse off under engine.

Keep reversing and rock boat from side to side (called sugging *this can also be used in conjunction with kedge).*

Try poling off using spinnaker boom, boat-hook etc.

Crew member(s) hang over end of main boom and swing outboard to list boat.

Stop engine, put on lifejackets, jump over-side and push; one man to remain with boat.

If these actions fail then immediately lay out kedge anchor. Even if a pull on the kedge warp does not free the boat it will at least prevent it being blown harder aground while the next set of operations are tried. These are:

Lighten the boat by loading heavy weights and crew into dinghy, lowering the anchor and cable onto the bottom, pumping water tanks etc. Haul off using kedge warp and engine together.

Heel boat further by securing a light anchor on masthead line and burying the anchor well off the beam. A second line looped to a mid point on this line will enable crew to list boat.

Cautions If, to lessen weight on sheet winch, a purchase or series of purchases are used in conjunction with the kedge warp, remember that nylon rope can part without any audible or visible warning and whip back with tremendous energy. If using engines, watch for signs of overheating due to blocked or obstructed filters and intakes, also sand being drawn into cooling system. Finally, if it is evident that nothing will shift the yacht, the weather is worsening and the position is dangerous, you should consider calling for assistance early, while there is still sufficient water for rescuers to reach you.

Precautions to be taken if boat cannot be freed:

Discover how long boat will remain aground and whether she will dry out completely (use 'Twelfth's Rule', see page 88).

Investigate sea bed to establish whether boat can be laid down on her bilge or will need to be kept upright with legs.

Deep keel boat; range anchor cable or similar weight along deck to ensure she lays facing away from incoming sea or deep water.

Clear rocks or obstructions beneath bilge and prepare a cushion of materials. A wind increase which coincides with returning tide may bring waves to damage through pounding.

Take out kedge to furthest limit and bury if necessary. If bad weather threatens lay bower anchor also.

Load heavy weights into dinghy, also batteries.

Pump bilge, secure gear below, shut off sea-cocks.

Secure deck hatches, seal with rigging tape, plug fuel and water tank breather pipes, vents and engine exhaust.

Fig. 2.   Long-keel boats are generally deeper aft. Crew forward directly she touches, boat may be reversed clear under power

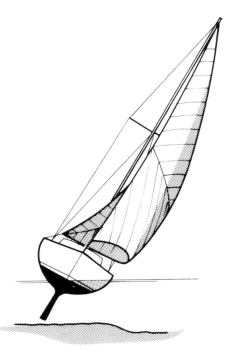

Fig. 3. An effective method of reducing the draught is to lower sail and have a crew member swing out on boom end

Fig. 1. A deep-keel boat which goes aground may be slewed off by going about smartly, backing the jib and getting the crew to leeward

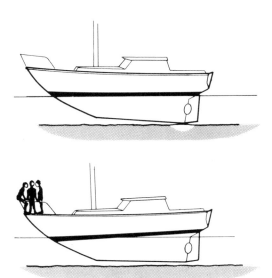

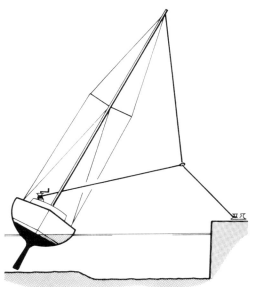

Fig. 4. Boat can be forcibly heeled with mast line

Fig. 5. Boat must be laid towards shallow water and protected from incoming sea

Fig. 7. Booms, spinnaker poles or legs securely lashed to keep boat upright on rocky bottom. Kedge anchor bow and stern prevents boat ranging to and fro when tide returns

Fig. 8. Surf can lift and pound a boat to pieces against rocks or hard sand. To save the hull it may be better to scuttle her by leaving seacocks open. Put out as much ground tackle as possible and remove equipment, machinery etc

Fig. 6. Everything prepared should flood tide bring worsening weather. Bunk mattresses, fenders, sail bags, etc wedged under bilge prevent damage through pounding by the action of the waves; heavy weights lowered into dinghy to lighten vessel; cockpit covered to prevent sea entry; hatches battened and sealed with rigging tape, sea cocks shut off; kedge anchor with chain cable in position

ANCHOR — Dragging

Circumstances and surroundings usually offer a clue as to cause and thus suggest the best course of action.

If anchor drags shortly after boat has turned with the tide it has probably 'tripped' and should soon bury itself. *Standby with engine or sail and be ready with kedge in case anchor has fouled.*

Anchor drag accompanied by sudden strengthening of wind, increase of current, or rise of tide probably indicates insufficient cable has been veered. *Pay out more cable.*

Drag due to poor holding ground may be improved by paying out more cable but do not be caught again. *Be prepared to start engine, make sail and shift to another ground.*

If compelled to stay; *lay second anchor in clear patch by causing the boat to sheer away from her bower anchor; use rudder, or engine and rudder. (Alternatively carry second anchor out in dinghy)*

If impossible to lay separate anchor; *back up bower anchor by securing kedge anchor on same cable and lay them in tandem.*

Check against anchor dragging; *be on hand when tide turns, take shore bearings, or if shoreline is obscured use watch lead.*

ANCHOR — Fouled

Anchor may be fouled or simply dug in hard; investigation, local intelligence or reference to the chart may tell.

If anchor is dug in hard:

Heave cable short, make fast and use scend of the waves and the boat's own buoyancy to break the anchor clear.

Sail or motor past the anchor to give a pull from the opposition direction.

If anchor has fouled ground chain etc:

Heave cable short (as much as you can get) and let go suddenly! This sometimes shakes the obstruction clear.

Use grappling hook.

Send swimmer down to pass rope underneath the chain and so hold it in a bight from on deck while anchor is lowered and freed.

If all else fails slip the cable and mark with buoy for recovery later. Also mark position accurately on the chart.

Fig. 9. Watch lead; the hand leadline is lowered onto the bottom with sufficient slack to allow for yacht's sheering, yawing and tide effect. If the yacht begins to drag, however, the line will become taut and lead ahead. (Useful when shore bearings are un-obtainable

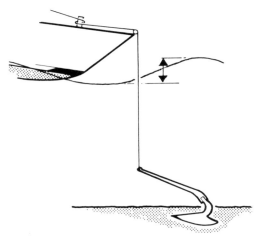

Fig. 10. Using the scend of the waves to break anchor clear

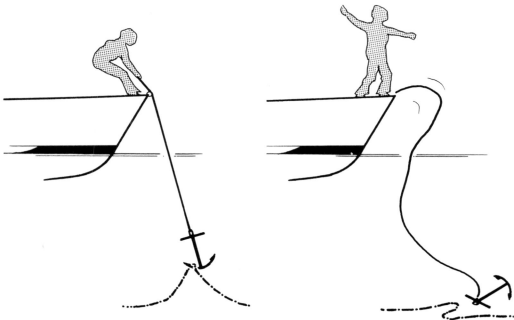

Fig. 11. Try clearing obstruction by heaving cable in short and letting go suddenly

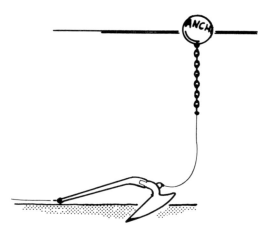

Fig. 12. A short length of chain, or weighted plastic sleeve, equal to the boat's draught, will ensure tripping line does not foul keels or propellers when anchoring over rocky ground

ANCHOR — Mooring

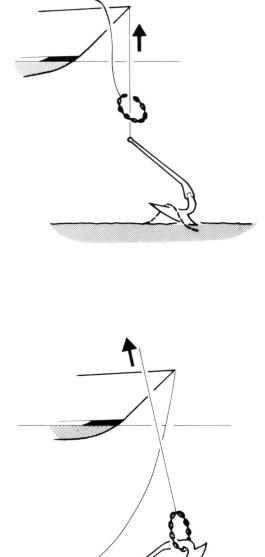

Mooring with two anchors is sometimes done in narrow waters to reduce swinging arc and prevent vessel grounding, obstructing main channel etc. (It is not recommended in crowded anchorages.) In tidal waters the anchors are laid in line with the current, the main bower anchor facing the stronger current.

Methods

Carrying out kedge: *Anchor in the normal way to main bower. Bend kedge warp to chain cable on deck and lower into water until the knot is well below keel depth and cannot obstruct. Take out the kedge anchor astern in the dinghy.*

Running moor with the tide: *Stop boat short of anchoring position, lower kedge over the stern, veer plenty of warp and sail on past the anchoring position. Lower bower anchor onto the bottom veer cable and heave in the warp until a mid position is reached. Make fast.*

Unmooring: *Take in slack cable first.*

Fig. 13. Method of clearing a fouled anchor with a ring of chain. Heave cable short, lower chain on an independent line to fullest extent. Slack away cable, heave up on chain

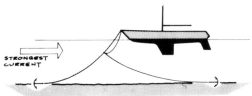

Fig. 14. Moored with two anchors; kedge taken astern in the dinghy

ANCHOR — Snubbing

Snubbing is the 'straightening-out' of the cable caused by strain imposed by wind or waves and is important to guard against especially with chain cable in sea conditions. It is seen, felt or heard as a juddering and can result in the anchor pulling out or the cable parting.

Preventions:

Veer more cable

Slide heavy weight on a line to hang from the bight of the cable. This increases catenery or sag.

Start engine and keep motoring gently ahead.

Use patent elastic snubber, a motor tyre, or a length of nylon warp secured between chain cable and boat.

ANCHOR — Yawing

Boats anchored with nylon cable are particularly prone to yaw (swing around madly). The long term remedy is to increase the length of ground chain which will in turn increase the inertia and create more 'drag' over the sea bed. More immediate remedies:

Lower a dead weight (sentinel) on a line and suspend it from the bight of the anchor cable.

Drop kedge anchor over the stern and keep line short so that the kedge will drag over the ground. The friction of this will reduce the tendency to yaw.

Hoist mizzen or reefed main and sheet it flat amidships.

Moor with two anchors.

Try steering.

(*See also*: CHAFE).

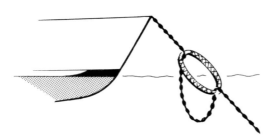

Fig. 15.   Precaution against snubbing

ANCHORED — Boat Rolling

Rolling at anchor can be minimised by the following proceedures:

Secure rope from boat's quarter onto anchor cable. Veer small amount of cable and adjust taut at LW. It may also help to hang weights in the bights to prevent the boat ranging about at high water and keep her close alongside.

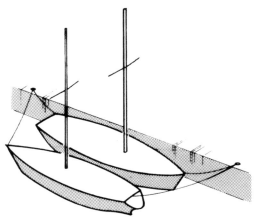

Fig. 19. Moor alongside other vessel so that crosstrees cannot foul. Use independent warps. Bow and stern arrangement ensures more privacy

Fig. 18. Large tidal range, weights hung from bow and stern lines keeps boat alongside and spares the need for endless adjustment

BERTHING ALONGSIDE OTHER BOATS

Choose neighbours of compatible type and size; try to ensure freeboards are equal height. Larger boat should lay inside.

Moor so that rigging and crosstrees cannot foul if boats disturbed by wake of passing vessels.

Moor independently; springs and breast-lines only to be placed on neighbouring boat, head and stern lines must be taken ashore.

If fender squeak a nuisance, smear with liquid detergent.

Enquire when inside boat intends to depart.

BERTHING ALONGSIDE — Drying Harbours

Drying out is a perfectly satisfactory arrangement providing the right precautions are taken. The boat must be listed slightly (about 10°) towards the quay to prevent her from falling over. This is done either by ranging weights such as cable along the deck, or suspending weights from a mast-head line made fast on the quay. Additionally a line can be passed around the mast and made fast on the quay to use as a preventer. It is also important to see the boat does not lay too far off the quay or, when taking the ground she may lean inwards too heavily with damaging results.

Another precaution is to ensure that the ground beneath the berth is safe, reasonably level and free from obstruction. If the boat is deeper aft then berth with stern in the deepest water.

The boat should be watched down — at least for the first time. Establish with the 'Twelfth's Rule' at what hour this will happen. Be prepared to rig hull support lines on delicately balanced fin keel yachts and restrict crew movement at moment of grounding.

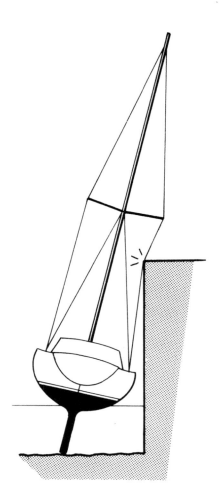

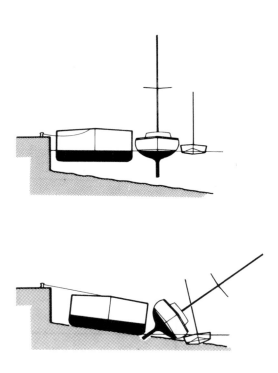

Fig. 20. Keep boat close to the quay to prevent rigging damage

Fig. 21. Beware of the flat bottomed barge, it draws very little and at low water will slide away from the wall. In drying berths never moor alongside other vessels and do not allow others to moor outside of you — includes your own tender

changes appreciably, a close quarter situation will arise.

Make bold and early alterations of course so as to leave the other in no doubt as to your intentions. At all other times it is important to keep as straight a course as possible.

Avoid passing close under a large vessel's stern, because the wake can be violent. Try to meet bow wave head on (warning those below in the galley).

If close quarter situation is imminent, make as much noise as possible; bang buckets, fire guns, horn, whistles, bells (shouting is useless), and turn away at best possible speed. At night, shine powerful torch at the ship's bridge, fire flares (but not to land on ship's deck), switch on cabin and deck lights.

Precautions in shipping lanes The limitations in manoeuvrability, the restrictions on vision and their overiding concern to avoid one another makes a large concentration of shipping extremely dangerous for small craft. Treat with the utmost caution and follow these rules:

Avoid crossing the path of ships at night and clear the area altogether in conditions of reduced visibility.

When necessary to cross, do so at right-angles, motor sailing if need be.

Post extra lookouts and have everybody dressed ready, with lifejackets to hand. (It is unwise to clip on safety harnesses in these circumstances.)

Signalling equipment ready, radar reflector hoisted.

Engine on tick-over or ready to start in an instant.

Ports, hatches, and doors ready to close or closed.

Dinghy ready to launch or towed.

It should be realised that even in clear conditions a small craft, with sea as its background, is very difficult to see from the bridge of a large ship.

Work out your own horizon distance and memorize it.

(*See* APPENDIX).

BRIDGE CLEARANCE

When information about bridge heights, tidal rise etc is uncertain or not available then this very approximate estimate procedure could be used to ensure safe mast clearance. Select a yacht with mast height considerably more than your own and position your boat at about 100 metres or yards from it. (This distance is chosen as being the amount of manoeuvring space you would need to turn the boat fully round, even under the most difficult conditions). Stand in your normal steering position in the cockpit and line up the other yacht's mast with your own. Mark with tape the points on your mast where the other yacht's waterline and mast top come. These are your guide marks. When you are 100m [100 yds] from the bridge check that the distance between the marks appears to fit under the bridge with a safe margin to spare. It must be stressed that this method is reliable only so long as the height of eye is the same (the marks could not be used by crew of different height), and that the judging distance from the bridge must never be less than 100 metres or yards.

In an emergency, when the boat is being swept under a bridge and all other attempts to check her have failed try using whatever power remains to position the vessel sideways. The hull offers much less resistance beam-on and as the upper shrouds strike the bridge, the boat should roll over to one side. With luck the mast will hold.

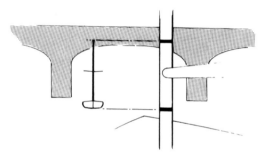

Fig. 29. Gauging the clearance with previously marked points on the mast

CAREENING

This is the age-old practice of forcibly hauling a vessel down on her beam ends to effect underwater repair etc. It used to be done in places where no docking facility existed or where a small tidal range made drying out impossible. Today it can be used for jobs such as anti-fouling, centre plate, rudder and propeller repairs and inspection, even repairs to mast and rigging. Suitable also when testing for leaks above the waterline.

Preparations The day should be calm and the waters protected. The area chosen should not be invaded by the wakes from passing vessels. All reasonable precautions should be taken against accidental flooding by shutting seacocks, cockpit lockers, hatches and doors and sealing with rigging tape where necessary. Ventilators should be capped, engine exhaust and tank vents blocked and both engine oil and bilge water pumped dry. The batteries should be taken ashore, the boom secured and the tiller lashed amidships. Beamy boats or boats with deep draught and high ballast ratio will be easier to haul down if some of the internal ballast or weights are moved to the heeled side. Generally the more weight that can be removed, the further the boat can be careened and the higher she will ride.

Careening alongside This is the obvious choice. The boat should be positioned parallel to the quay at a distance about equal to three-quarters the height of the mast and should be held bow and stern with long warps. It will help to heel the boat and hold her steady if the anchor (use two anchors on larger boat) is brought aft under the boat, the cable secured to the deck on the side facing the quay and the anchor laid off well amidships. A 4 : 1 purchase sent aloft on two halyards should haul down the average 6 tonner. Heave down gently avoiding jerks and keep an eye on mast and rigging. Once the boat is careened work can be undertaken from the dinghy.

26

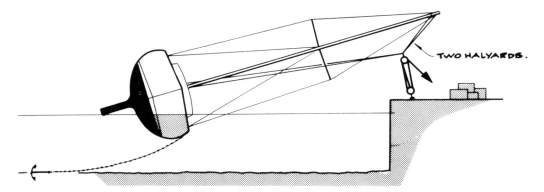

Fig. 30. Careening alongside. Boat is held off with long bow and stern lines plus anchor(s) led under the boat and away from the quay

Careening fully afloat This can be done between pile posts or while anchored head and stern. The same preparations apply but here a weight will have to be employed. The most expedient weight is a drum suspended from a masthead tackle and filled with water. As the drum weight increases so it is hoisted aloft by a masthead tackle and at the same time allowed to veer away from the boat's side by a control line. The drum will adjust its freeboard to provide the necessary downward force so that boat and drum will be kept in equilibrium.

(The exact amount of water to be put into the drum can only be found by an experiment but as a guide a 230 litre [50 gallon] drum filled with water weighs 227 kg [500 lbs] in air and this is heavy enough to haul down a 27ft keel boat.)

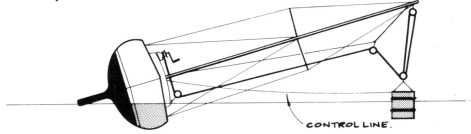

Fig. 31. Careening fully afloat. Heeling moments are applied cautiously by hauling the drum aloft, allowing it to veer away from the boat's side while at the same time adding more water to the drum with hose pipe and bilge pump. Empty drum slowly with syphon or screw bung

CHAFE — Prevention of

Aloft Protect sails from chafe by:
Taping spreader ends and placing rollers (or tennis balls) around cap shrouds above.
Keeping mainsail off spreaders when running.
Not allowing sails to flog more than necessary, especially in calm conditions with swell running.
Using kicking strap or boom vang when running and reaching (or boom fore guy).
Using shroud rollers (place also around inner forestay if applicable).
Using a rope topping lift.
Taping rigging screws.

Running gear Protect by:
Providing sheaves with generous radius (the diameter radius of sheave to rope should be 5:1).
Using swivel blocks for leads rather than bulleyes etc.
Providing good, fair leads which keep sheets clear of guardrail and other obstructions.
Having well rounded and large sized cleats, the horn variety are best.
Turning halyards and sheets end for end occasionally.
Using longer sheets than necessary, splicing the sail fastening arrangement off-centre and when localized wear begins to show, shifting this position progressively towards centre to minimize wear.

Mooring warps Protect by:
Preventing warps from 'sawing' against each other.
Parcelling with canvas or providing a sleeve of plastic hose where rope passes through fairlead.

Splicing a sleeve of plastic hose into the eye of each warp.

Cushioning sharp edges or inadequate fairleads with fenders or other material.
Replacing 'soft' eyes with shackles and thimbles when laying up afloat.

At Anchor:
Employ a 'riding stopper'. This is a short length of chain with a rope tail used to transfer the weight from the anchor warp where it passes over the fairlead. The rope tail is made fast to the anchor warp with a rolling hitch while the chain is simply looped and dropped over the samson post.

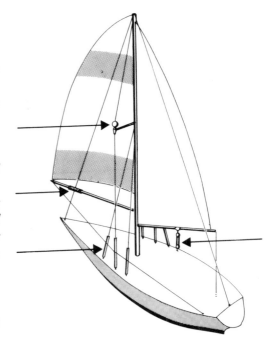

Fig. 32. Areas most prone to chafe and precautions to guard against it

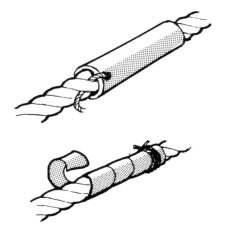

Fig. 33.   In some circumstances it is necessary to protect a rope at the fairlead

Fig. 34.   Laying up afloat in a marina requires extra precautions. Thimbles and shackles are an insurance against chafe in winter gales, comforting also for the owner who is absent for long periods

Fig. 35.   Alternative method of fastening riding stopper to rope cable

DISABLED BOAT TO SAFETY

In conditions of no wind a disabled boat can be moved to safety by any of the following methods:

Dinghy as a tow-boat If the dinghy has an outboard engine secure and tow alongside for better control. If towing under oars use a long towline to prevent 'snatching'.

Sweeps and sculls Very large boats can be moved with sweeps or sculls or even punted if the water is not deep.

Warping The boat can be moved towards a safe destination by taking warps to conventient strongpoints (buoys, dolphins, quay walls etc) and heaving towards them. The warps can be taken off in a dinghy or they may be floated down wind or down tide with fuel cans, fenders, lifejackets etc to buoy them to where others may be able to make them fast.

Kedging If there are no available strong points use the dinghy to lay out a kedge anchor and kedge the boat in stages.

Drudging This consists of lowering the anchor onto the bottom and allowing the boat to be carried stern-first with, or across, the tide. The anchor snubs over the bottom to control the boat at a safe speed while steering stern first using small amounts of helm. To stop, veer more cable and hold on. (Secure warp to anchor crown and use upside-down or substitute weight if anchor flukes are in danger of fouling ground moorings etc.)

Tide sailing Even without wind it is possible to move the boat across the tide under sail by employing the small amount of wind caused by tidal movement. Position boat abreast the tide and sheet sails on uptide side.

(*See:* ENGINE FAULTS, PROPELLER FOULED, WARPING, KEDGING, JURY RIG).

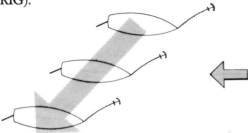

Fig. 36. Moving across a current by means of lowering the anchor just onto the bottom and making cable fast; rudder is also employed. Called 'drudging' it can also be used to manoeuvre the boat directly downtide

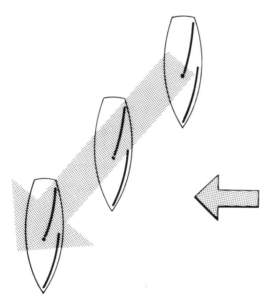

Fig. 37. Tidal sailing; progress made by putting the boat square onto the current, setting the sails and utilising the small amount of wind which is generated

DISMASTING

The immediate danger is of hull damage caused by the mast being thrown against the boat by the force of the waves. Until the rigging can be cut free or the rigging screws let go, the mast must be kept to leeward — it will probably have fallen on that side anyway — and at all costs should be kept clear of the rudder and propeller. A wooden mast can be made to act as a sea anchor and keep the boat's head to wind thus minimising rolling while the trouble is sorted out. Whether it will be possible to salvage the mast and lash it alongside the guardrails will depend upon the circumstances prevailing. Similarly, circumstances will decide whether you can reach port under engine or whether you must construct a jury rig. In this case it will be necessary to salvage as much of the rigging as possible, even if it means having to jettison and buoy it for recovery after the immediate emergency is over.

(*See also*: JURY RIG).

DISTRESS

Rescue services are limited and, in coming to your assistance rescuers may be unable to give help to somebody whose need is more urgent. Do you require rescue or simply a tow? (The signal for *I require assistance* is V, flag or by lamp). Is your difficulty something which you could remedy yourself, given time and a cool head? Consider these points before summoning help. If you decide danger to life exists, call help *early*.

Visual Signals Read instructions on rockets and flares, they vary in methods of use and ignition. Make sure they are held vertically the correct way up, ignited well clear of the sails, fired from over the side and pointed away from the vessel downwind. Use wisely, it may pay to wait until approaching ship's lights are seen or there is known to be shoreside activity etc. High altitude rockets may not be seen with low cloud ceiling. Fire in groups of two at short intervals. The first may only be glimpsed, the second provides a positive sighting and chance for an alerted observer to take a compass bearing. Use newer rockets first then follow up with older stock using greater caution. If the outside casing is damaged or suspect, do not use the rockets under any circumstances.) A signal from on shore consisting of a rocket throwing three white stars or orange smoke (by day) is confirmation that the coast guard have seen you. Be prepared to use two or more of the recognised distress signals at the same time. (Solitary signals have been misinterpreted or ignored.) Recognised distress signals for small craft include:

Rockets or flares showing red lights.
Smoke signal giving off orange coloured smoke.
S.O.S. signalled by torch or whistle.
Gun fired at one-minute intervals.
Continuous sounding of fog signal.

Smoke from burning oil-soaked rag held in a saucepan.
Clothing hoisted aloft or attached to an oar and waved.
Erratic behaviour such as motoring in figure-of-eights or hoisting sails up and down.
Square flag with ball or bundle exhibited above or below it.
Ensign upside down.
International code signal flags NC.
Slowly and repeatedly raising and lowering outstretched arms.

Radio telephone distress procedure:

1   Set to International Distress frequency 2182 kHz (or Channel 16 VHF).

2   Transmit alarm signal (if fitted) for between 30-60 seconds.

3   Transmit call: MAYDAY MAYDAY MAYDAY.

4   'THIS IS . . .' — name of vessel repeated three times (spell with phonetic alphabet if necessary).

5   Repeat again MAYDAY, name of vessel, position (distance and bearing from nearest landmark), nature of emergency and assistance required plus any other information which might facilitate rescue.

6   Listen for acknowledgment.

Emergency position indicating radio beacons These are small, buoyant transmitters which automatically send out a distress signal on VHF frequencies for up to about 48 hours. They can be used from on deck or in the water. They are continuous and provide a homing facility.

ENGINE — Lifting Out

The average boat's engine can be lifted quite easily with the aid of a pair of sheerlegs. Check engine weight with handbook. Small auxiliaries may be lifted with the mainsheet tackle, others may need additional purchase. A rough estimate for power needed to lift a particular weight is as follows:

One man can pull about 55 kg [120 lbs], so multiply this by the number of men employed and the number of parts of rope in the tackle, this roughly equals the lifting capacity to hand. For example: two men with a 4-part tackle can lift about 550 kg [1,200 lbs]. Spinnaker boom and main boom can be employed as sheerlegs if nothing else is available. Secure together with a figure-of-eight lashing at the head which will tighten as the legs are splayed apart. A strop to carry the tackle is passed around this lashing. Keep the legs as close together as is practicable; the narrower the spread the less will be the strain in their parts. The legs should rest on wooden pads on the deck and to prevent any accidental movement they should be secured in position with heel ropes.

Sheerlegs have a limited amount of swing before becoming unstable. Once the engine is hoisted, move it aft in stages. Have bearers placed across cockpit sides ready to lower the weight, while the position of the legs is moved.

Use the sheerlegs to lower the engine over the side or use a plank to slide the engine up or down to the quay side.

Fig. 38. Lifting out with rig employing boat's gear. Sheerlegs have limited swing, weight is traversed in easy stages so leg positions can be shifted

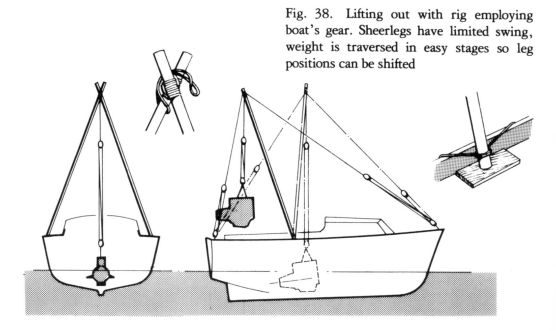

FATIGUE

It is only in comparatively recent years in the study of accidents, that proper acknowledgment has been given to the contributory effect of human fatigue. In yachting the usual causes such as prolonged activity, anxiety, discomfort and motion sickness are always present and fatigue is always a possible hazard. The effects of fatigue are obvious. What is not so obvious is the way in which fatigue will play tricks on the senses, qualifying wrong decisions or allowing them to pass completely unnoticed. It is necessary to watch and anticipate the danger signs of fatigue both in oneself, and in others, (absentmindedness in routine jobs is an early sympton), and be prepared to question every chosen course of action.

Under extreme circumstances the onset of fatigue may have to be accepted. If anchoring or heaving to are impractical the yachtsman can only carry on, aware of his impaired mental abilities, and subsequently checking and re-checking (even debating aloud) his every decision. He should try to keep an accurate DR plot going as this is an insurance against acting upon rash and improbable conclusions. He may even have to resort to a chemical stimulant for the times when sustained and additional effort is required, say, for example, when trying to make port. But beware, such stimulants are effective for a prescribed period only, after which a state of near unconsciousness may ensue. They should be used only with extreme caution.

Prevention

Fatigue can be prevented by setting yourself, your crew and your boat easy and attainable targets. It can be lessened by eliminating anxieties, by having adequate sleep, shelter, warmth and food. In definitive terms consider and carry out the following points. Plan all passages in accordance with the stamina and experience of your particular crew. With a family crew this may mean the extent which you yourself can comfortably endure.

Consider the weather. A previous 'good day's sail' when repeated as a beat against a rising gale and drop in temperature may quickly wear down the crew's reserves.

Always provide alternatives when planning and do not commit yourself. This especially applies with respect to arranging rendezvous; the need to drive on because you promised to meet a friend off the ferry at a certain time is inviting trouble. So too the necessity to be back at work on Monday!

Do not be afraid to disappoint the crew when a promised visit or voyage has to be cancelled by circumstances or a change in the weather.

Eliminate as many unnecessary anxieties as possible by ensuring that every item aboard the boat is sound or functioning properly.

Know your boat. Confidence in your handling of her and in knowing how she behaves in bad weather will reduce anxiety which leads to fatigue.

Establish a watchkeeping system suited to the conditions and capability of the crew.

Make sure that off-watch men rest and sleep whenever possible; a crew that sits up to admire the fading harbour lights will be spent by the early hours.

Hot food and drink are essential; they may have to be prepared beforehand and kept in vacuum containers. Warm and protective clothing, shelter in the form of side screens, dodgers or cockpit hoods are equally important.

Make all possible provisions to minimise seasickness as this accelerates fatigue.

FIRE FIGHTING

A fire needs *fuel*, *heat* and *oxygen* to sustain it. The more you can do to limit and eliminate these factors then the quicker the fire will be extinguished and remain extinguished.

Oxygen An extinguisher is the primary tool for shutting off oxygen by smothering the flames with gas, foam or dry powder. However, oxygen can also be restricted by covering the fire with blankets, by closing doors, ports and hatches, by stopping the vessel or steaming downwind.

Fuel Prevent more fuel from reaching the fire by removing obvious combustible items; in the case of petrol, diesel and gas this means shutting off supply at source. Ensure these valves are always accessible and that everyone aboard knows where they are.

Heat This can most effectively be removed with water. Even when flames have been extinguished do not ignore this; an engine casing heated to several hundred degrees can quickly cause re-ignition unless the heat source is removed. Damping down is

fundamental to successful fire-fighting. However, it is unwise to use water as a primary extinguisher where engine fuels or gas are concerned unless a fine spray can be employed. The jet of water merely breaks up the burning particles and spreads them through the boat.

Fire-fighting techniques A fire must be properly fought; it is no good simply pointing the extinguisher at the fire, pulling the trigger and expecting the fire to go out. Get as low and as close as you can to the seat of the flames (shield your face with your arm if need be). Make sure you hold the extinguisher upright and attack the flames immediately in front of you using a 'sweeping' action. Work from the front of the fire towards the back. With a fuel blaze it is especially important to extinguish every particle of flame systematically as you move forward. If this is not done properly, any one of the small flames left can re-ignite the entire area once again. Also, once you have extinguished the foreground of the fire you will be able to move in closer to the seat of the fire.

Fires in engine compartments are best tackled from above with side hatches etc closed. This way the whole area provides an airtight bin where the extinguisher components can be contained and work effectively.

Speed is of the utmost importance in fire-fighting. Do not waste time trying to put out a potentially dangerous fire with a small aerosol extinguisher. These are intended only for small fires. On a large fire they are useless.

Every boat should carry at least two 1.5 kg [3 lb] dry powder extinguishers placed in the most strategic and accessible positions.

In addition the boat should have a smothering blanket or aerosol extinguisher for dealing with small fires.

Tests have shown that when the extinguisher case looks worn the contents too are likely to be in poor condition. Replace the extinguisher with a new one.

Fire drill:
Raise alarm.
Have extinguisher ready
Shut off fuel supply.
Exclude draught by closing ports, hatches, steam downwind.
Fight fire with extinguisher.
Dampen down.

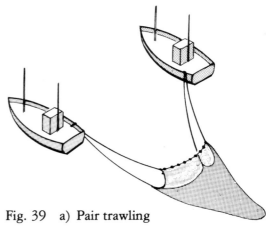

Fig. 39   a) Pair trawling

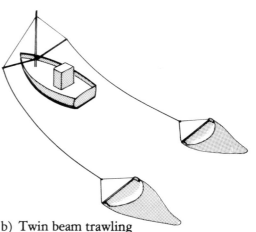

b) Twin beam trawling

FISHING VESSELS AND WHAT TO EXPECT

When engaged in their occupation with gear and nets in the sea, fishing boats have absolute right of way. To cause them to take avoiding action might result in serious injury or expensive damage. Unfortunately, because of the varied ways of fishing and the different manoeuvres employed it is sometimes difficult for the yachtsman to know how best to act. The following describes the more popular fishing methods and the usual manoeuvres of the vessels which use them.

Trawling
Trawling is the action of dragging a net through the water. It is carried out sometimes by a single vessel, or sometimes by vessels working in pairs 50m [160ft] apart.

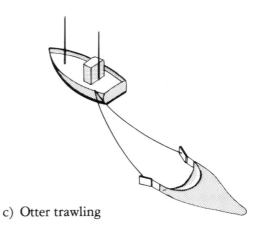

c) Otter trawling

Signals By night: green light over a white light. Additionally a white masthead light and sidelights may be shown if the vessel is making way. Pair trawlers usually shine searchlights on their trawl. By day: two black cones, points together, one above the other. Under 20m [65ft] these may be substituted with a basket hung from the forestay.

Action *Single trawlers have trawl on weather quarter so pass to leeward for preference, otherwise pass well clear under their sterns and watch for a cod end buoy. Speeds can be deceptive — even a small vessel can trawl at 4 knots. Pair trawlers are fast, especially the large stern trawlers. Expect a trawler to turn and reverse its course suddenly at the end of a run.*

Drifters

Drifters usually work in large clusters at night. They lie stopped, either stern-to or stem-to their nets which can extend up to 3 km [2 miles] to windward of the vessel. The outer end of the net is normally marked with a dan buoy and light. The nets hang

vertically in the water suspended from buoys.

Signals By night: drifters show a red light over white with an additional lower white light in another part of the boat to indicate the direction of the net. This applies to vessels with nets of more than 150m [500ft]. Sidelights and sternlight may be seen. When hauling or shooting nets the deck will probably be illuminated with deck lights. Drifters sometimes hoist a mizzen sail to keep them head to wind. By day: a basket is hoisted on the forestay although larger vessels will show two black cones with their points together. If gear extends more than 150m [500ft] a black cone, point up, will be shown in direction of the gear.

Action *Pass to leeward. If compelled to cross nets then do so with caution keeping a careful watch for buoys. Usually nets are suspended at a safe distance below the surface, between 3 to 5m [10 to 16ft] but this cannot be relied upon implicitly. Beware of damaging nets and fouling propellers.*

Fig. 40.   Drifter

Longliners

These are customarily encountered over rocky patches which are inaccessible to trawlers. Baited lines with hundreds of hooks are used and may well extend over 2 km [1 mile] approximately from the vessel which is usually anchored. The craft are invariably small and may include ex-lifeboats

etc which can sometimes be mistaken for drifters.

Signals At night: red light over white. By day: a basket hung from the forestay.

Action *Pass ahead for preference, upwind or up tide. Longliners can, however, be passed reasonably close on all sides.*

Seiners

A popular method of commercial fishing, there are several variations but basically it involves the use of a huge bag net suspended in the water from buoys. The vessel shoots the net with a buoyed rope and dan buoy at the end and then proceeds to steam around in a wide circle to close the net.

Signals In close proximity a Purse Seine vessel may show two flashing yellow lights in a vertical line.

Action *Give a wide berth and watch for buoys on the surface. Vessel may either be turning in a wide circle or may be stopped downwind hauling her nets.*

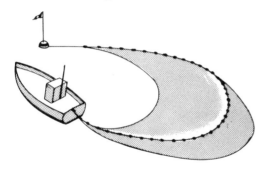

Fig. 41.   Purse seiner

Crabbers

Pots for crabs, lobsters, crayfish etc are left unattended. The lines are buoyed, usually in trots along the depth contour lines parallel with the coastline. In strong tide conditions these buoys may be dragged under the surface where they present a hazard to propellers, particularly at night. Buoys are rarely marked. To avoid them it is advisable to go further offshore. Fishing boats attend pots during daylight hours. Keep well clear for they manoeuvre erratically.

Note:
Fishing boats have absolute right of way *only when fishing*; do not be unduly influenced by their signals which are sometimes misused.

FOG

The existence of fog may be determined by 'breaks' in the sea horizon, by 'feathering' or by haze around the navigation lights at night. The following precautions should be taken:

Hoist radar reflector.

If possible get good position check before fog clamps down.

Start prescribed fog signal (providing the boat is under 12m [40ft] in length, this may be an efficent sound signal at intervals of not more than two minutes).

Post lookout forward, away from engine noise.

Reduce to moderate speed so that the vessel can be stopped if in danger of stranding or collision.

Small vessels are advised to clear shipping lanes and make for shallow water where risk of being run down is minimised. Anchoring may be advisable. If impossible to clear shipping lanes, then:

Muster all crew on deck with lifejackets but do not hook on safety harnesses.

Have dinghy launched or ready for immediate launching.

Preserve boat's buoyancy by closing all hatches, windows, ports and doors.

Keep engine on tick-over to maintain steerage way.

If the engine is noisy, shut down occasionally and listen for fog signals. Try to establish compass bearings of approaching ship's fog signals. If the bearing does not appreciably change and volume increases then sail away at right angles as quickly as possible.

Change watches more frequently to maintain vigilance. Keep quiet.

If making for harbour then endeavour to close the land at right angles and take frequent soundings; listen for sound of breakers, cliff echoes, traffic noise, etc as these may provide only clue to shore proximity.

FOG — Navigation

Dead Reckoning Everything depends upon the accuracy of DR positions; keep the plot going and use echo/sounder, log and Radio Direction Finder to assist. Pay careful attention to accurate steering and if the speed is reduced allow for greater tide effect. Remember the longer the passage in fog the less reliable the DR position will become.

Soundings Position finding will be helped if the boat is kept in soundings or deliberately steered over areas of marked contrast such as dredged channels, deeps or banks. It may also be helpful to follow a contour line running parallel with the coast where the constant depth ensures a safe distance off. Use also 'Line of Soundings' method to establish position in fog.

Point to point In the right circumstances there is great advantage in proceeding directly between one landfall mark and another. If the mark is seen or the fog signal heard the boat will have a regular check on her position. However, it requires careful navigation and on each leg a pre-worked ETA is needed so that the boat can stand off should the mark not materialise when expected.

Buoy hopping Piloting from buoy to buoy in fog has obvious merits providing these precautions are followed:

Check on the identity of every buoy which is passed. Over familiarity with the waters can easily lead you to 'recognise' a buoy merely because it occurs where and when expected.

Steer by compass at all times. Again over familiarity with the area or a (temporary) lift in the fog can lead to laziness. A slight change in the wind can make the helmsman alter course so that the buoy which appears ahead may not be the right one. Note tide effect at each buoy and make suitable allowances.

Work out the ETA of the next buoy you hope to see. Use the log line or table given here and a stop watch. If the buoy does not appear when expected, stand on for a further minute and then turn and make a pattern of shallow zigzag crosses over your original course until the buoy is found.

Log line or table

Use the table opposite for checking time between buoys. The distance between buoys is expressed in cables (⅒th of a nautical mile) and this is found by measurement on the chart. The speed is the estimated speed of the boat in knots.

Example: If the distance between two buoys is 6 cables and the estimated speed is 4 knots then the expected buoy should show up in 9 minutes.

Fog signals Sound signals in fog can not be relied upon. The distance at which they may be heard will vary enormously and the apparent direction can be misleading. There can be occasions when the signal is completely inaudible, or at other times it may be possible to hear the higher note of a two-tone fog signal but not the lower note, or vice versa. There are almost a dozen different fog signal sounds used for navigation marks so be sure to know which one you are listening for.

(*See* APPENDIX).

Remember: Fog demands that you act with patience and proceed cautiously; be prepared to take the long way home (which will often turn out to be the shortest) and accept that usually the wisest plan is to get into shallow water, anchor and wait for the fog to clear.

		Speed in knots								
		1	2	3	4	5	6	7	8	9
Distance in cables	1	6	3	2	1½	1¼	1	¾	¾	¾
	2	12	6	4	3	2½	2	1¾	1½	1¼
	3	18	9	6	4½	3½	3	2½	2¼	2
	4	24	12	8	6	4¾	4	3½	3	2¾
	5	30	15	10	7½	6	5	4¼	3¾	3¼
	6	36	18	12	9	7¼	6	5¼	4½	4
	7	42	21	14	10½	8½	7	6	5¼	4¾
	8	48	24	16	12	9½	8	6¾	6	5¼
	9	54	27	18	13½	10¾	9	7¾	6¾	6
	10	60	30	20	15	12	10	8½	7½	6¾

GOING ALOFT

Bosun's Chair This is the quickest method. Reeve a gantline through the mast-head block (or use main halyard if strong enough), and have crew on deck haul you up while you either assist or steady yourself against the mast. The disadvantages of the bosun's chair are it's dependency on outside factors; the condition of the block, the skill of those on deck, (especially if a winch is used), and the fact that they may not hear your commands properly. As a general rule it is better employed by experienced crews who are used to working together.

If a bosun's chair is not available a small plastic fender makes a more comfortable seat than a bight of halyard.

Self-lowering hitch Use this knot both to secure yourself aloft and to control descent; it relieves the need of unskilled hands tending you from below and gives greater self-dependency. It also allows you to climb aloft single handed. The knot can be difficult for unpractised hands, in which case it is advisable to work aloft in stages; make the knot near the deck and adjust as you progress holding the two moving parts tightly in one hand and feeding through the slack line with the other.

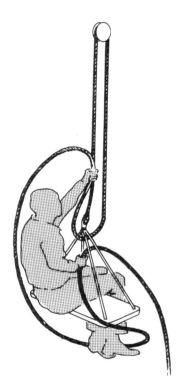

Fig. 42. Self lowering hitch; enables a man to climb and lower himself single handed

Temporary ratlines This involves tying a series of short lengths of line between the shrouds to use as footholds. The lines are secured with rolling hitches and sufficient slack has to be left to allow the jamming action of the hitch to work properly. On stainless steel wire it may be necessary to tape the shroud first to prevent the hitch from slipping. Above the crosstrees the ratlines are continued between the mast and forestay.

Rope Ladder Make a series of large over-hand knots in a mooring warp and hoist this up to the crosstrees on a halyard (or use two halyards). Twist the rope several times around the mast to hold tight in position and secure the lower end. Climb the mast using loops as footholds. To go higher, stand on the crosstrees, hoist ladder and repeat operation.

Jacob's Ladder Make one using a number of wooden 'rungs' secured to the bight of a mooring rope with marlinspike hitches. Hoist aloft on halyards and once again work in two operations, first to the crosstrees then above.

Working aloft makes heavy demands on mind and body which means it is sometimes difficult to think clearly. Thus it requries considerable forethought and planning. Inspect the job from on deck with binoculars, decide how you will tackle it and what tools you require. Tools should be placed in a bag or a bucket (not plastic, these are unstable) and either secured to the bosun's chair or sent up separately on a halyard. Bundle remaining halyards together to assist climbing. Do not trust small, light halyards or winches, do not stand up in the chair. If there are snap shackles on the halyard use them to secure the spring lock with rigging tape. Explain to the crew what you intend to do.

At sea, remember that movement on deck will be greatly magnified aloft. Protect yourself against chafe or burns by wearing long sleeves, long trousers (even lifejacket and sea boots if necessary). Have a line on the chair with which you can secure yourself aloft, or at least a line running down to the deck which can be wrapped around the mast to hold you steady. Wear a safety harness if

Fig. 43.   Rope ladder made from mooring warp

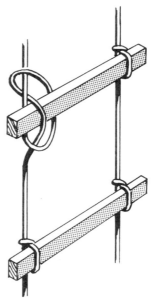

Fig. 44.   Extempore rope ladder made from mooring warps and pieces of wood; can be hoisted aloft on halyards

practicable. Select the most comfortable course, the most reliable helmsman and choose suitable sail rig. If only a marlin-spike is to be used then secure this to your wrist with a lanyard; at night tape a torch to your forearm.

HARBOUR PLANS

It is impossible for a cruising boat to carry large scale charts or harbour plans for every port she might someday wish to enter. It is therefore worth remembering that a workable harbour plan can be constructed by scaling up the outline of a particular port shown on the passage chart and filling in with information given in the pilot books. Where practicable, construct the drawing on the small scale chart in the sea area close to the intended harbour. This way, it is handy for reference while the bearings and distances used to make the plan can be taken direct from the compass rose and latitude scale. The scale in the example illustrated, the port of Mourilyan in Australia, was

Fig. 45. Blow-up of harbour shown on passage chart, embellished with information from pilot books provides a helpful picture of what to expect when making unscheduled stop-offs

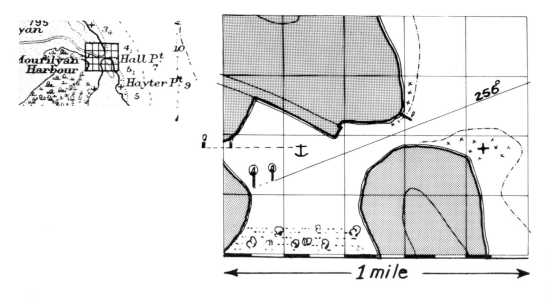

1:30 which means that a mile on the chart is 30 miles on the plan and that conveniently makes one cable's length on the plan equal to 3 mintues of latitude.

For an accurate drawing, first construct a grid over the harbour and then increase the scale of the grid for the plan, draw in the coastline square by square. Next draw a latitude and longitude and with these as datum points, plot the positions of the important features such as lighthouses; you will find that the positions of buoys, dangerous rocks etc are frequently given relative to these. It will be necessary to search the pilot book fully before you are able to extract all the relevant information you require. Enter each detail and notice how finally it all fits together like a jigsaw puzzle. Try also to visualise distances as you plot them and relate these to familiar items. You will discover that by the time your plan is complete, you will know the harbour very well.

HALYARD ADRIFT

Halyard adrift in a strong wind:
Slow boat to reduce apparent wind.
Turn to bring errant halyard over the fore and aft line of the boat.
Try to grab with boathook.

If unsuccessful:
Secure a length of fishing line, weighted with a small shackle, to the end of the boathook and use as a whip to twirl around the end of the halyard.

Halyard out of reach:
Make a large marlinspike hitch in the bight of an adjacent halyard. Haul aloft and try to manoeuvre the bight of this over the stray halyard end. If successful, pull the knot tight by jerking the line and this should then grip itself around the halyard end enabling it to be hauled down on deck.

Tie a short length of line to an adjacent halyard with a rolling hitch and hoist aloft until the knot is well above the stray halyard end. It may then be possible to 'plait' the doubled parts around the halyard and get sufficient grip on it to haul it down.

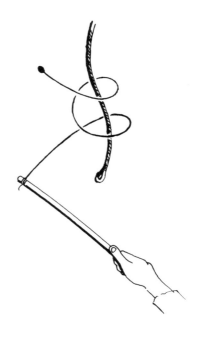

Fig. 46. Capturing an errant halyard with a whip . . .

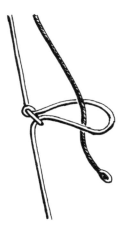

Fig. 47. — with a large noose . . .

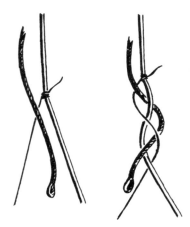

Fig. 48 — or by 'plaiting' two other ropes around it

HEAVING TO

This is a means of stopping the boat so that she will lay quietly enabling the crew to rest, take nourishment, find their position, wait for daylight and so on. It is less trouble than anchoring, frequently more comfortable and almost always more practicable. Moreover it has the safe advantage that the boat retains her manoeuvrability and can be sailed off in an instant.

Each boat will 'hove to' in its own way depending on type, hull shape and rig. This again can change when an increase in wind demands sail change, a reef and new sheeting positions. The owner must experiment to discover how best the boat heaves to under varying wind strengths.

Most boats are made to heave to by sheeting the headsail to windward and lashing the tiller to leeward. The backed headsail then tries to force the bows to leeward while the tiller attempts to turn the boat into the wind. With the mainsail still carried, these counter actions result in a slow movement, mainly to leeward but also slightly ahead. It is called drift.

The rate and direction of drift will depend not only upon hull profile, type and rig but also on size and sheeting of sails, the amount of sail carried, and the wind strengths. It can be negligible or, in a good wind with all sail set and sheeted in hard, it can be in excess of 2½ knots; tide or current can increase (or nullify) this. Generally the rate of drift is of secondary concern and the aim is to get the boat comfortable hove to. There are several ways to get a boat to heave to, the following have been used successfully:

Headsail backed, tiller lashed to leeward, both sails sheeted in hard.

Same as above except that one or other or both of the sheets are eased.

Tiller lashed to leeward, jib handed or reduced, mainsail freed off.

Tiller lashed to leeward, jib backed, mainsail reefed or handed.

Lying 'a hull', all sail handed, tiller lashed to leeward.

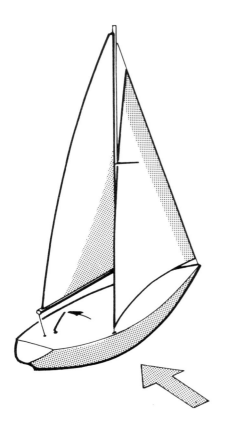

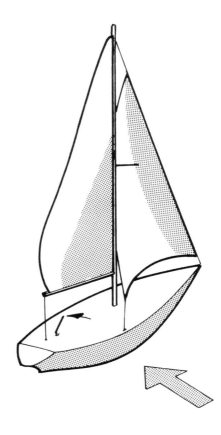

Fig. 49. Hove to with both sails sheeted in hard. Comfortable but expect high rate of drift. Some boats may heel excessively and reefing may be helpful

Fig. 50. Main and fore sheets eased. Reduced drift but sails may flog in strong winds. With sails freed off the boat will probably drift more to leeward

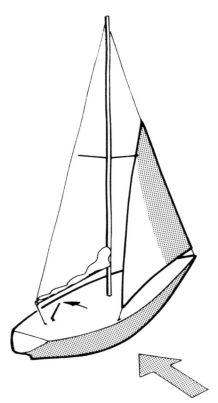

Fig. 51. Hove to with mainsail handed or freed off completely. Little drift but probably less comfortable

Fig. 52. Hove to under mainsail alone. Drift will be minimal but motion less comfortable. Sail prone to flog

As a rule the more sail the boat can be made to carry and the harder it can be sheeted home then the quieter she will lie. However, this will certainly result in a faster rate of drift; she may also heel excessively. A boat hove to under headsail or mainsail alone will drift very much more slowly (and more to leeward) but she will be less comfortable and the sails may flog badly. Lying 'a hull' with all sail lowered and tiller lashed to leeward with elastic cord is an extreme measure performed only in heavy weather.

Note

A vessel hove to is still 'under weigh' as described in the Regulations for the Pretion of Collision at Sea, unless she carries 'not under command' signals. Therefore all the steering and sailing rules still apply and she may be expected to give way as directed. However, where choice exists it is preferable to heave to on the starboard tack as this gives right of way over other sailing vessels in the majority of cases. Moreover it is easier to prepare food and drink if the galley is on the port side.

HEAVY WEATHER

(The following is specifically directed towards the small family cruising boat with family crew as these are considered to be at greatest risk).

Experience has shown that left on her own the typical modern family cruiser can survive in the heaviest seas. If conditions become too bad and the strain on the small crew unbearable then they would be advised — earlier rather than later — to stow all sail, lash the tiller to leeward, get below and batten down. The motion will be violent but so long as the boat can be kept watertight she will be safe, her buoyant and beamy shape will enable her to ride over the waves like a bottle.

Searoom It is vitally important that if the crew do decide to let the boat lie a' hull then she should be given plenty of searoom, and that means open sea with a regular pattern of waves. Areas of banks and shallows can create dangerous waves both above and in their shadow. Obviously every effort must be made not to allow the boat to drift into areas such as these nor indeed onto a lee shore. Estimate the amount of searoom needed; a boat lying a' hull may be expected to drift at the rate of 2 knots and a coastal gale be expected to last between 24 and 30 hours (although a wind shift within this period is almost certain).

Shipping As big a risk is the danger of being run down. Small boats become hidden in the wave troughs and accompanying rain squalls make both visual and radar observation uncertain. If shipping abounds it will be prudent for the family cruiser to run her engine and the boat be helmed into the seas.

This way she will have manoeuvrability and could at least get out of the way, something which would likely not be possible with sails. In shipping lanes, hoist radar reflector, exhibit masthead light, have flares and torches ready.

Keeping the vessel watertight This is absolutely vital. Boats with large windows or those set in rubber grommets are the most vulnerable. Where possible, rig storm covers on the outside and, should a window be stove in, be prepared to plug with cushions, sailbags etc. Cap ventilators, put on canvas hatch covers and keep a watchful eye on all openings and skin fittings.

Crew It is equally essential that the small family crew to not exhaust themselves or reduce their stamina by needlessly trying to sail the boat (especially in a reckless bid for shelter). A cold, tired and seasick crew can quickly loose heart and will become too lethargic to make decisions and cope with emergencies. For this reason, the small crew are advised to heave to early, either under reduced canvas or with all sail stowed. Keep up morale and strength with hot food prepared early and placed in vacuum flasks. The crew on deck should wear safety harnesses.

General preparations Reef early and progressively. Be especially watchful under following wind and sea conditions when wind strengths may be deceptive. Problems may be encountered when reefing and it is better to sort these out before worsening conditions make deck work difficult or impossible. Stow or lash all gear above and below deck, rig lifelines, fix position and keep DR plot going based on estimated drift. (Throw a buoyant — but not wind blown

— object over the side to help calculate drift.)

Small cruiser behaviour The typical fat, family cruiser cannot be expected to make anything to windward in rough water or wind conditions above force 6-7. She may make some progress under engine with just enough sail to steady her (too much heels the boat and makes the propeller ineffective). Otherwise, with reduced sail boats of this type do little better than hold their ground — although this may be all which is required. It should be possible for the boat to *reach* in winds up to gale force and also to run downwind, but again, when running beware that the boat does not carry more sail than can be safely handled. In strong winds a jib is usually sufficient. Shallow draft boats in particular can be difficult to hold on a run, it is better to tack downwind and avoid the danger of broaching. The risk of broaching can be reduced by streaming warps although this is of questionable benefit for the small, tubby cruiser which in any case will probably not have the necessary size and length of warp required (at least 100m [100yds] approximately of 16mm [⅝in] nylon towed in a bight). Mooring warps are useless. Moreover, a great deal of sea room is required; a boat may still make in excess of 5 knots towing warps. But above all it must be remembered that sailing the boat, and especially downwind, is going to tire the crew and this is something which must be avoided. Heaving to is much the wiser consideration.

Limited searoom The boat may hold her own by sailing under storm jib and trisail, or reaching may be possible. A sea anchor will not eliminate drift entirely because it depends upon a certain amount of drift for

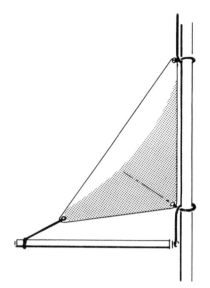

Fig. 53.   Jib used as a trisail

its efficiency. It will, however, keep the boat's head facing into the sea. (An extempore sea anchor can be made by bundling together such items as mattresses, tyres, doors, oars, etc and streaming them on a line over the bow. They will also need to be weighted.) The favoured method for a small family cruising boat to reduce leeway or even get to windward is to run the engine at slow speed and helm the boat to keep her shoulder into the sea.

(*See*: WAVE BEHAVIOUR, HEAVING TO, OIL TO CALM SEAS).

Note:

1   If engines are used in rough weather the excessive rolling may cause tank sediment to enter lines and cause breakdown. Keep tank and filters clean.

2   If forced into unscheduled harbour through stress of weather remember to re-notify authorities, friends or relatives of change of plans.

KEDGE ANCHOR —
Laying out with Dingy

Rope warp should be as long as possible, flaked down and carried in the dinghy — not fed out from on board. Carry kedge secured over the dinghy transom — this is the safest and most stable position. Lower carefully when in position, do not throw it overboard as the rope may foul anchor or snare. If the vessel is aground lay out kedge immediately to prevent the boat being blown further ashore. Place towards direction of deep water and incoming sea.

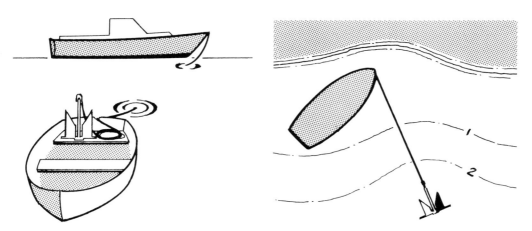

Fig. 54.   Laying out the kedge anchor

JURY RIG

Endeavour to make up jury mast using remaining parts of old mast fished together or combined with items such as dinghy oars, boathook, spinnaker or main boom. Wooden parts can be joined with 'splines' lashed around the mast and tightened with wedges. Aluminium extrusions can have wooden spar inside for additional stiffening and to prevent compression when outside lashings are applied. Consider using also metal sleeve from section of mast.

Staying the mast and getting sufficient and equal tension on all parts of rigging will be difficult. Be prepared to use block and tackle, Spanish windlass and various frappings, plus whatever rigging screws are remaining.

Securing the sail A number of grommets may have to be made up and sewn into the sail so that it can be laced to the mast and boom.

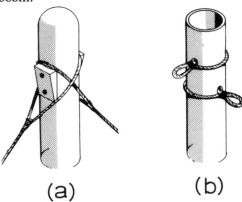

(a)   **(b)**

Fig. 55. Securing rigging to a) wooden mast and b) metal mast

A Bipod mast has many advantages. It will probably be stronger, more easily stayed and much easier to raise. (Raising a jury

mast with a small crew in the open sea can present one of the biggest problems.) If the bipod mast is rigged with a wire set up hard between apex and deck centre position then the genoa can be hanked to this and used as a mainsail.

Spritsail rig This rig has several advantages: it permits almost any 'square shaped' piece of sailcloth or canvas to be used; it is loose-footed which means the boom can be included in the mast fabrication (an oar or boathook is used for the sprit); it gives a generous spread of sail aloft while keeping the centre of effort low down; it can be scandalised and the sail furled away quickly should the boat be beset by a squall, and finally, the sprit itself can be used as a cantilever to raise the mast into position.

The rig can be incorporated with a jib and a mizzen (mizzen mast stepped in the main hatch).

(*See*: KNOTS AND LASHINGS FOR EMERGENCIES, MAST RAISING AND LOWERING, SAIL REPAIR).

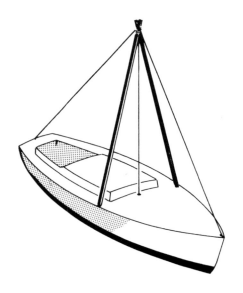

Fig. 56. A bipod jury mast

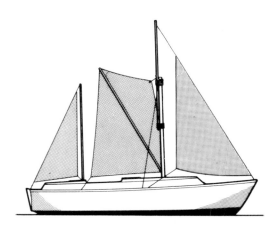

Fig. 57. A spritsail rig

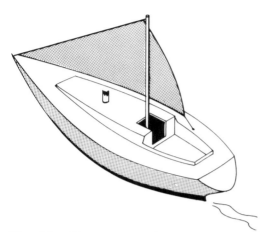

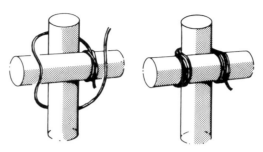

Fig. 60.   Square lashing

Fig. 58.   Genoa set on jury mast stepped in main hatch

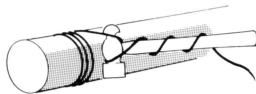

Fig. 61.   Method of applying tight wire lashings

KNOTS AND LASHINGS
FOR EMERGENCIES

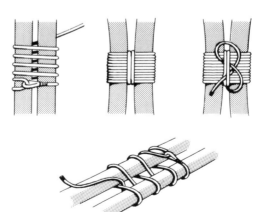

Fig. 59.   Applying a strop (for extra pur-chase on kedge rope etc)

Fig. 62.   Racking and seizings (used for fishing broken spars together)

LANDFALL — Making a

As a general principle it is better to sail from feature to feature than from port to port. Choose something which is easy to identify as your landfall, high land, a lighthouse, a light vessel, a headland or some other salient point. Then, when absolutely sure of your position, turn and make the run down the coast to your final destination. Approach unfamiliar land at right angles. An oblique approach can easily lead to grounding. Navigational aids are designed to be recognised from seaward and may be obscured to the observer approaching at a narrow angle along the coast, (perhaps when tide dodging?). Buoys and beacons marking off-lying dangers may also be missed. A right angle approach across the depth contours will give a sharper indication of position as soundings are taken. Hold off to windward for as long as possible. It will be easy to drop downwind in the final stages of an approach, but not so easy to claw off should an ill-chosen approach take you into difficult waters.

Try to get a good position fix in advance of a landfall. This is particularly important by day. Use RDF, sextant, soundings and combination of all three and continue on same course until a feature point is positively identified. If a position fix is unobtainable then rely on previous DR and compass course. Do not alter course on assumptions drawn from vague shore outlines. On a flat or unfamiliar coast the best time to approach is a few hours before dawn when navigation lights will be seen at their maximum range and provide positive identification and position check. Close to land in daylight. Study chart and pilot book beforehand so as to better recognise natural features and navigation marks. If a lighthouse is the landfall point then what is the colour and where is it sighted? Is it on the top of a cliff, half way down, or at sea level? How high is it in comparison to the cliffs? What does the chart indicate about buildings, vegetation, background hills, promontories etc? What does the pilot book say about colours and the shape of navigation marks? What about colour of the cliffs? Is there a sharply defined beach? Would you expect to see any early discolouration in the water due to the presence of a river? Might there be floating vegetation far out to sea? Are there any smells associated with the area? Is there a marked change in the wave pattern — something that is quite evident in the lee of an island? Can the land be seen reflected in the clouds? At night, is there some nearby town whose lights will illuminate the sky? Are flying insects noticeable? A proliferation of land birds? Is there an increase in traffic? Are there any fishing boats or ferries which are known to have connections with the port? You see, there are many features to take into account.

LEAKS

Once located, the inrush of water from a large and potentially serious leak may be minimised by throwing the boat onto the opposite tack, by sheeting in the sails to heel the boat, by stopping or even going astern on the engine.

The fast and immediate rise in the level of water within the confines of the narrow bilge may suggest that the leak is more serious than it actually is. Once the leak is well under water the inrush will be less and the level might be held quite comfortably by the bilge pump.

First attack the damage from inside, breaking away furniture and using any available material to plug the hole; clothing and bedding stuffed into polythene bags or sail bags are probably most handy. Place a board over the area and shore off with suitable lengths of timber, using sufficient pressure merely to hold them in position. Now get sail off the boat.

A 'collision mat' is the obvious choice to plug the hole from the outside although the

'wine glass' shape of the yacht may make it impossible for this to lie flat against the hull. A mattress wrapped in a sail — or even better a foam backed carpet — provides a good cushion effect and is probably the most effective. Secure it around the hull with as many lines as required and heave tight with blocks and tackles, frapping turns, Spanish windlass etc.

If a collision mat proves impractical, the hole will have to be patched. Polythene sheeting adheres reasonably well to a wet glass fibre hull or the kind of tape used for repairing leaky water pipes will also hold onto a smooth surface under water. Alternatively, a light patch made up of a chart wallet or Terylene fabric could be held down with rubber mastic. A more durable patch made from plastic material, (such as the lid of a sandwich box), could be secured to the glass fibre hull with bolts or self-tapping screws — if conditions are such to permit a man to go over the side in a bosun's chair or rubber dinghy. Bed the patch down on mastic or a piece of blanket soaked in grease.

Other leak-stopping materials that might be considered include cotton waste, softwood plugs, oilskins, seaweed, soap and butter.

Tracing small leaks This can be a long and tedious business. First look in the obvious places — keel bolts, skin fittings, chain plates, stern tube, rudder fittings, engine, toilet and any thru-deck fitting. Try to localise the leak area by blocking off bilge limber holes and discovering in which part of the boat the water gathers. Test and inspect for leaks while making way at speed, while heeled, with a pressure hose or by careening. Consider controlled tests with dye added to water.

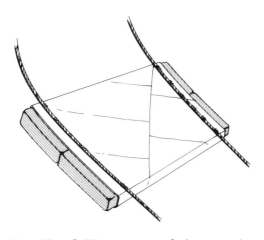

Fig. 63. Collision mat made by wrapping a sail around a foam mattress

LEVELLING A HULL

LIFELINES

If building or alteration work is to be carried out it is vital that the hull is first levelled. Begin with the fore and aft line. Take a length of clear (or reasonably clear), plastic hose and secure the ends, one at the bow and one at the stern. The ends should be above the waterline marks which should already have been identified. Fill the hose with water until it reaches the higher (or lower) end of the waterline. Adjust the fore and aft trim of the boat by using wedges until the waterline marks at both ends correspond to water level. Top up the hose as necessary. The same method could be used to level hull athwartships.

When rigging lifelines remember they may have to bear the weight of two men, not just one! Ringbolts should be thru-bolted and an 8mm [1in] diameter nylon rope should be used. Where possible, arrange lifeline on both sides of the boat with little interruption and keep always to the windward side when moving along the deck. Safety harness lines should be about 2m [7ft] in length.

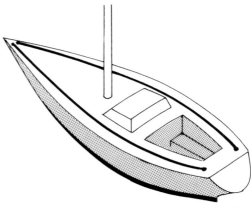

Fig. 65. Unbroken lifeline allows crew clear run without having to change. Disadvantage is that a longer line is invariably slack which then means two hands are needed to hook on

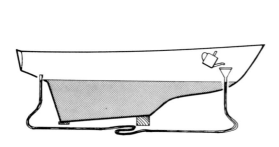

Fig. 64. Setting up in the fore and aft line

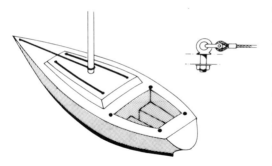

Fig. 66. Ringbolts in each corner of the cockpit allow crew to hook on before leaving cabin. Helmsman's safety line will need to be shorter than those of the rest of the crew

MANHANDLING A TRAILER

The unique construction of a boat trailer provides a perfect — almost frictionless — lever which can be used to good effect when manoeuvering by hand. Place a block behind one wheel to prevent it running back and push the tow-hitch end of the trailer in a sideways direction; some forward progress will be made. Now place the block behind the wheel on the opposite side and swing the trailer back; still more progress is made. Continue this 'pumping' action but to make things simpler use two wooden blocks and secure them one behind each wheel with lanyards. This way, they are pulled behind the wheels and placed in position automatically.

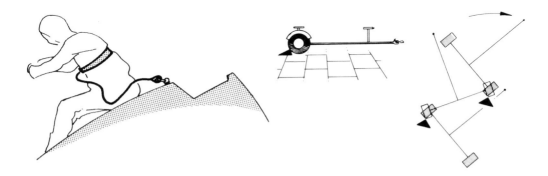

Fig. 67. Sit down when working and hook-on to windward

Fig. 68. Trailer is slewed from side to side

MANHANDLING A BOAT ASHORE

A shallow draft boat, bilge keeler, multi-hull and some motor boats, can be man-handled ashore using blocks and tackle. A level pull is necessary and this will mean having to erect a post (unless a tree is handy). Back up the post with stays secured to stakes driven into the ground or buried anchors. Dig the bank away if necessary and provide greased planks or rollers under the keel. The hauling line should be secured around the hull or deckhouse as the samson post alone is unlikely to be strong enough.

(*See*: MOVING HEAVY WEIGHTS).

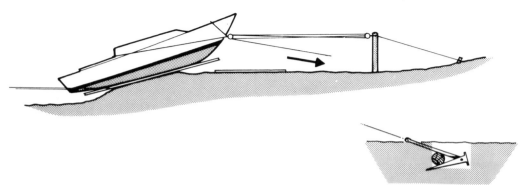

Fig. 69.   Anchor used as a strongpoint

MAN OVERBOARD

This is one of those occasions where a practised drill takes charge because senses may be momentarily stunned. The drill which you have instilled into yourself may not always be ideal for the particular circumstance but this is of less importance. What does matter is that it will cause you to do *something* positive and, once begun, your shocked state will quickly return to order.

The drill is: *Turn*, *Shout*, *Lifebuoy*, *Look-out*, *Lee side*. Say these words over and over again until they are imprinted on your mind.

Turn The classical manoeuvre in a sailing boat is the swift *gybe*. This gets the boat downwind of the man in the water and, by the time it has completed the circle the boat will return head to wind, close alongside the casualty, ready to pick him up. Gybing is not practical in all cases.

Shouting This will alert those on deck, those below and even perhaps other boats. It may also give some reassurance to the man in the water.

Lifebuoy Try to aim and throw this within the man's reach. A lifebuoy is also a marker. If you are towing a dinghy it may be sensible to cast this adrift.

Lookout If there is more than one person left aboard, he or she should be instructed to keep their eye on the man overboard while the boat is being turned. This is far more important than lending a hand with the necessary sail manoeuvres. In a rough sea or poor visibility, a moment's distraction in the lookout's concentration may result in the man in the water being lost.

Leeside It is vitally important that the boat be brought into a safe position *downwind* of the man in the water. Engines should also be stopped. Should a person fall overboard unnoticed, then the boat must be returned to search on the reciprocal course under engine. If difficult to turn immediately then mark the wake by throwing a string of items over the side, turn around and steam through them; this ensures you are in original track. Make allowance for leeway and/or compass deviation on the previous course.

Picking the man up Take the urgency out of the situation either by placing a rope under the person's shoulders and securing him to the boat or by placing a lifebuoy into his hands secured with a line to the boat. Either will lessen anxiety and give you time to prepare for the lifting procedure. There

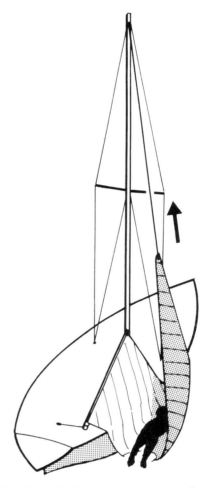

Fig. 70. Hoisting an exhausted or unconscious man

have been cases when a casualty has been towed in shallow water because lifting proved impossible.

Methods of getting a man aboard:
Lower ladder, weighted bight of rope, or tyre fender to provide a foothold.
Inflatable dinghy; if carried on deck in half-

inflated condition, then launch and allow him to scramble into this.

Drop mainsail, free from mast track, cast off topping lift and drop boom in cockpit, bundle sail over the side so that the man can climb in and be brought aboard in the belly of the sail, by heaving on the halyard. Heave as boat rolls; cut away guard rails.

Hook on halyard to his safety harness.

MAST RAISING AND LOWERING

If the mast is stepped on deck and hinged in a tabernacle it ought to be within the crew's own capability to raise or lower it. In the absence of a high quay wall, a bridge, or a large ship to lay alongside and the obvious advantages of height they offer, an arrangement using the boat's own gear can be employed. This must be something to act as a cantilever to steady or pull the mast during the critical part of the hoisting or lowering operation. It is essential to keep the mast from swaying from side to side. To prevent this, the most stable arrangement is to have two booms lashed together in an 'A' frame. They should be lashed at their heels to the chain plates. In smaller boats a ladder or even a dinghy launching trolley can be used as these are both reasonably stable. A single strut can be employed although it will need to be very securely stayed.

If the mast is high then a topping lift led

beneath the spreaders will provide a better lead. In small boats however it is customary to use the forestay as a topping lift. The lifting power is provided either by fixing the mainsheet tackle to the head of the booms, or, by using a single line led through a block on the stem-head and onto the windlass or winch. Before hoisting it is precautionary to secure the backstay and also the after set of shrouds.

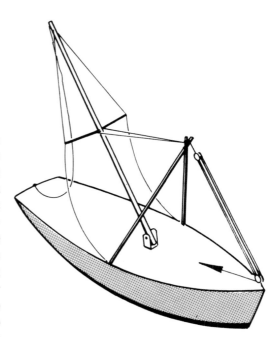

Fig. 71.   Hoisting mast with sheerlegs

It is possible for two-masted vessels to use their mizzen masts to heave up or lower the main. If the mizzen is small then it would be wise to provide temporary strength by lashing a spar to it and rigging extra backstay preventers. If booms and spars are not

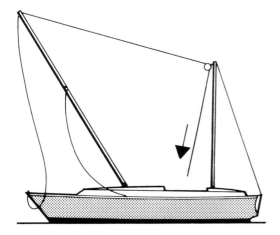

Fig. 72. Using the mizzen mast

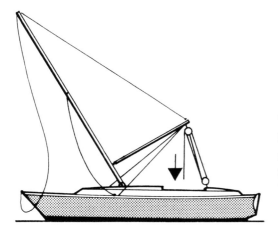

Fig. 73. Using main boom, topping lift and mainsheet

available then it is also possible to raise or lower a mast by using the main boom and goosefitting arrangement. The boom will have to be well stayed. In both instances the mast will be raised or lowered over the bow so it will be necessary first to moor in a

position where the crew will be able to stand ahead of the boat to support and see the mast down.

MOVING HEAVY WEIGHTS

With no mechancial power to hand, and little outside help, it is still possible to move remarkably heavy weights without injury using traditional seamanship methods and 'tricks of the trade'.

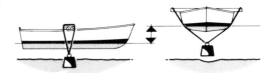

Fig. 74. Flotation: heavy weights can often be floated or rafted from place to place (see Appendix for Buoyancy) or raised with the lifting effect of the tide

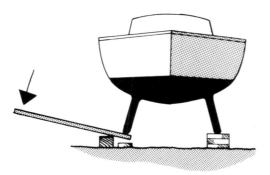

Fig. 75. Levers: a strong plank or pole has a powerful lifting effect; it can also be used to assist when sliding heavy objects

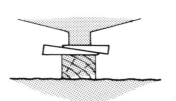

Fig. 78. Block and tackle: for extra power rig to advantage with the hauling part leading from the moving block. Remember you can increase the power still more by clapping an additional block and tackle on the hauling part. (Or leading it to the winch)

Fig. 76. Wedges: for a safe and steady lift few things match the power of a wooden wedge. To prevent splitting aim to strike the wedge at the right angle corner where the grain is longest

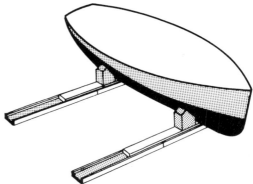

Fig. 77. Jacks: not a traditional seamanship tool but a fairly commonplace object

Fig. 79. Greased planks: reduce surface friction when sliding

Fig. 80. Rollers: for smaller items tabular plastic fenders make a good substitute

Fig. 83. Sledges

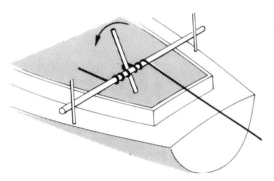

Fig. 81. Spanish windlass

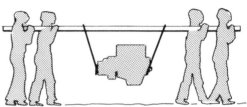

Fig. 84. Friends

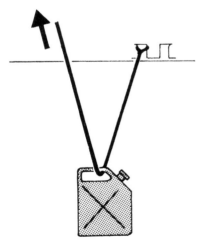

Fig. 82. Parbuckling: the advantage gained is 2:1

NIGHT PASSAGE

With a new crew or a strange boat it is better to set sail in daylight and let darkness come on gradually, rather than put out at night. It makes sense also to avoid any areas which require tricky navigation such as unlit or rocky areas, headlands or fishing grounds (especially where pots and lines are used), tide races and shipping lanes etc. In general, stand further offshore at night.

Watches of two hours duration are considered the best with the most adult and experienced man keeping the middle watch.

This is when the efficiency and alertness of younger and less competent crew members is likely to fall off. The skipper should leave definite orders when to be called in respect of approaching ships, landfalls or questions of uncertainty.

Rig In all but settled conditions it is wise to reduce sail at night to a comfortable rig which one man can handle. Sails which restrict visibility or which are difficult to hand or reef are better not carried.

Navigation Keep the plot going. At night, one's senses play tricks, speeds seem faster, winds stronger and distance of lights curiously difficult to judge. Having a DR position to refer to will be a bulwark against rash or improbable decisions. Check characteristics of lights carefully. Searching for a particular light with a known period can lead to the false assumption that the light seen is the one sought. Use Rising and Dipping bearings to check distances from lights. Protect night vision by screening cabin lights. A torch carelessly shone in the helmsman's eyes may impair his night vision for over ten minutes. Use a red bulb for the chart light or shield it with red cloth.

Shipping Remember the range of big ships' lights and use this as an indication of their distance from you.

Binoculars seldom 'find' a light, they merely tire the eyes. Use them for identification and checking the period of a light after it has been seen by the naked eye. A good pair of night binoculars are 7 x 50. This gives a magnification of x 7 which is large enough to view the object without it being shaken too much, while 50mm will give a good performance in poor light.

OIL — for Calming Seas

The heaviest and thickest oils are the most effective, particularly vegetable and animal oils. A steady trickle onto the sea is all that is needed and this is usually achieved by having the oil in a small canvas bag (traditionally stuffed with oakum) and allowing it to seep out through holes pricked with a sail needle. Approximately ½ litre [1 pint] of oil an hour is all that is required. The greatest effect is in deep water. In extremely shallow water or breaking surf it has least effect of all, although it is still claimed to be of some use. In very cold water, the potential value of oil is very much reduced.

Application in small boats

Hove to The oil bag should be hung in the water on the windward side. As the boat drifts to leeward the oil slick will be spread upwind.

Running The oil bag is hung over the bow so that the slick is left astern where it will reduce the breaking crests. Unlikely to give good results unless wind is dead astern.

At anchor (or sea anchor) A boat riding to its anchor can fasten the bag on an endless whip attached to the warp or anchor buoy. This way, the oil is diffused well ahead of the boat and the bag can be hauled aboard for re-filling.

Towing Oil gives its best service in towing applications where it can dampen the waves and prevent the hawser parting. Hang oil bags on each side of the bow of the towing vessel so she may also have the benefit.

Crossing a bar (flood tide only) Oil has been used in aiding a vessel over a bar where seas have been breaking but in general terms its effects in these circumstances are uncertain and should only be considered by experienced men in emergency. Pour the oil into the water and allow this to drift over the bar ahead of the boat. The boat will then follow in towing an oil bag astern.

Alongside a wreck Providing that the wreck or crippled vessel is in deep water and there are no survivors in the water, oil poured into the water to windward beforehand will assist when attempting to get alongside. (In this application the direction of the current may have greater effect than the wind.)

OUTBOARD ENGINE DROPPED IN WATER

The shorter the period of immersion the less chance sea water (or to a lesser extent fresh water), has to corrode and destroy machined surfaces. Try to reclaim a ditched motor as soon as you can and then:

Drain off all the water by removing spark plugs and turning the engine over by hand. Do this with the engine first in the vertical position and then with it lying on its side.

Squirt oil into the plug openings and turn engine over by hand to lubricate the machined parts and bearings and reduce effect of corrosion.

Drain off fuel from tank and carburettor, refill with fresh.

Pump fuel through before re-assembling carburettor to ensure all contaminated fuel is flushed out.

Strip down magnetos and all electrical equipment, rinse in fresh water, clean and thoroughly dry.

Re-assemble, fit dry plugs and try to start the engine.

Allow it to run for about 15 minutes and while running squirt some oil into the carburettor to assist lubrication.

Stop the engine and change oil in lower unit which will have emulsified.

Note: Do not attempt to start the engine if it was dropped overboard while running at high speed as damage to cylinder walls may have been caused. Similarly, do not attempt to start the engine if the water in which it was immersed was heavily laden with silt, or the bearing and machined parts will become scoured. You would also be ill-advised to attempt to start high powered outboards which have sophisticated electrical systems. Take these to a dealer for thorough overhaul and cleaning.

PROPELLER FOULED

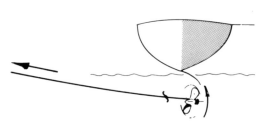

Fig. 85. Grab free end of rope (tie an extra length to it if necessary) and take as far astern as possible. Heave on the rope and turn the engine in the opposite direction. Turns should slide off propeller blades as the rope 'unwinds'. Caution: before turning over engine by hand switch off or remove plugs

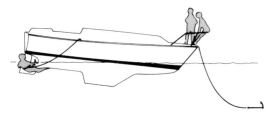

Fig. 86. Anchor, trim the boat by the head and send crew over the side to deal with foul-up personally. Beware: working under the boat's counter in sea or swell conditions can cause injury; make sure the man is attached with a lifeline. See also that engine is switched off and taken out of gear

Fig. 87. The compressed turns of a rope are easier to saw than cut. Use hacksaw blade or breaknife tied to broomstick

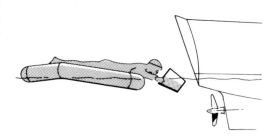

Fig. 88. An upturned and part-inflated dinghy makes a useful working platform. A plastic bucket with the bottom cut out makes for clearer viewing by eliminating surface ripples

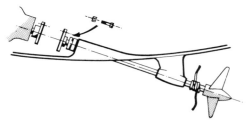

Fig. 89. Release coupling bolts and slide shaft back to loosen rope turns

RADAR REFLECTOR

Even a good radar reflector can be reduced to 50 per cent efficiency if it is not set up correctly. The proper position is shown in the diagram and is easily understood as the 'catch-water' position. The radar reflector should be hoisted as high as possible. The minimum recommended height is 4.6m [15ft]. It should be maintained in good condition and not masked by sails or gear. A damaged reflector loses efficiency, but a reflector mounted low behind wet sails with the boat heeled is almost totally ineffective. The minimum safe size is 400mm [16in] from corner to corner.

REEFING

A sail must be properly reefed for it to work at its maximum efficiency (the smaller the sail area the better it will have to perform), and also to prevent the sail from being permanently stretched out of shape.

Roller Reefing If the gear is efficient it is better to put the reef in while the sail is set and drawing. This results in a better shape with tighter rolls, reduced tendency for the leach to creep forward along the boom. It also helps to eliminate wrinkles and folds which might otherwise form if the sail were allowed to flog. A refinement, sometimes possible, is to lower the boom in the mast track, 'wind' it up with the reefing gear, and then lower the boom once more. In almost all cases it will be necessary to slow the boat by easing sheets etc.

See that the luff rope stows neatly around the fore end of the boom and that the sail banks are not strained in their trackway.
Keep the leach stretched aft. It will have a tendency to creep forward particularly if the boat has been stopped and the topping lift set up. Keep the rolls tight.
Remove sail battens.

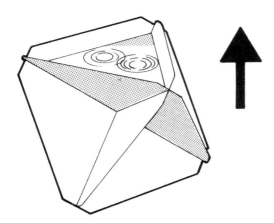

Fig. 90. The 'catch-water' position. Radar reflector should be hoisted so that, if its construction were solid, rain-water would collect in upper segment. Correct position for investigating radar beam to strike squarely into the corners and send back maximum signal

Signs of a badly set sail

Effect	Cause
Short and hard wrinkles radiating from each reef point	Reef points tied too tightly or reef cringles in leach and luff not drawn down far enough
Wrinkles at some reef points only	Tension uneven and some points have been tied too tightly creating hard spots. Slack off where indicated
Wrinkles at each reef point and a billowing in between	Leach has not been stretched far enough aft. There should be a slight fullness evenly along the foot
Long and pronounced wrinkles radiating from the leach	This condition accompanied by slackness in the leach indicates that the leach has been stretched too far aft

After three or four rolls most booms sag due to the uneven build up between luff and leach. This can be prevented by inserting tapered battens into the leach of the sail as it is rolled. Alternatively, a long wedged-shaped piece of wood can be fixed permanently to the underside of the boom.

Points of slab reefing
Never hoist or lower sail with the boom unsupported; the weight of this exerts a strain diagonally across the sail which can cause it to become misshapen. Use topping lift to raise the boom slightly. (In bad conditions do not take chances, secure in boom crutch or gallows, put boat under backed headsail and get mainsail off.)

Secure the luff first. Make sure that the reef cringle and tack cringle are drawn together and lashed.

The leach must next be stretched aft and the reef cringle secured as close to the boom as possible. The reef 'line' now becomes the foot of the sail. This means keeping it parallel with the boom and inducing the same tension.

Fold or roll up the surplus sail and tie the reef points starting from the centre outwards. If possible the reef points should be tied around the sail only, not beneath the boom. Tie the points with equal tension, do not tie too tight.

Use slipped reef knots and half hitches throughout.

To shake out a reef:

Haul in boom over the quarter and if necessary luff up.

Set up topping lift and lower the sail a little to get some slack.

Strictly in this order let go; reef points, leach and finally luff.

Hoist sail, free off topping lift, sail on.

RESCUE

By helicopter Make certain that the aircraft can identify you from other boats in the area; show hand flare, continue visible distress signal etc. Where possible, hold the boat on a steady course into the wind. If it is not possible to steam into the wind then stream sea anchor, (oars, furniture, weights bundled together will do), or even let go main anchor and cable to reduce surface drift. Try to indicate wind direction by streaming tapes from stern pulpit. The mast, sails and rigging of a yacht can impede hoisting operations and even cause serious injury. Drop sails, backstay, topping lift, aerials etc and be ready to let mast go overboard. Helicopter crew will show handwritten instructions from side hatch. They may order you to jump into the water; if so, do this one at a time and only on their signal. (Aircraft may have to carry survivors ashore one or two at a time.) If ordered into the water, wear your lifejacket, remove

your seaboots and hold on to the end of a line 10m [30ft] downwind from the boat. Do not secure yourself to this line. Alternatively, the helicopter crew may wish to hoist you from the dinghy, towed astern. In this case be ready to trail warps, oars, furniture etc from the stern of the dinghy to prevent wash from the rotor blades blowing it around. It is almost certain that a crewman will be winched down to assist in hoisting operations. Help him to get his footing and do not be alarmed by the electric shock you receive upon touching him, it is harmless and momentary. Help him to get his footing and out of the harness but on no account make the winchline fast. Have complete confidence in the helicopter crew who are trained for this job and do as you are instructed without argument or hesitation. On being hoisted up do not grab for the aircraft or the winchman inside but allow them to manoeuvre you inside.

By lifeboat Often, valuable time is lost by the lifeboat having to search for you. If you know the locality, know the lifeboat which should be coming to your aid and have some idea of its speed capability, so that you may know when to expect it to be close at hand. (In the United Kingdom, for instance, it takes about 15 minutes for the average lifeboat to launch by day, after being alerted by the coastguard). Guide the lifeboat to you by firing further distress signals. Under clear conditions at night a high altitude rocket can be seen for 20 miles.

The lifeboat coxswain may wish to take off crew or he may decide to tow your boat to calmer waters. His decision will be dependent on the sea conditions, the type of lifeboat and the likelihood of your sinking. Wherever possible a deep water lifeboat will attempt to tow so be prepared to secure towline (*see*: TOWING). Inshore lifeboats, on the other hand have limited towing capability.

Big ships will probably wish you to come alongside and may indicate this by Morse code. They will provide a lee for you. In rough conditions, they may additionally try to sheer and smooth the waves or they may spread oil. Remember, big ships are neither equipped nor suited for rescue. Nor are their crews trained in rescue work. You should make your own decisions. Unless the sea is moderately calm or the ship has a low freeboard and can be recognised as a particularly manoeuverable and well-manned vessel, (i.e., warship, ferry, passenger ship, buoy maintenance vessel etc), you would be well-advised to decline offers of help from very large ships — unless it is a matter of life and death! If, however, you decide to abandon and sea is rough then consider using a life raft as transfer vehicle. Under these conditions a yacht attempting to close alongside a ship is a highly dangerous manouvre.

here is practically guaranteed to clear it, but does take a little while to set up. Therefore it is advisable to go to it straightaway and not waste time on trial and error methods.

Method:

This technique uses the Spanish windlass principle and the tools required include a broomstick (or similar handle), a length of rope to use as a stopper and a marlin spike. Secure the end of the rope stopper around the base of the winch, or adjacent strongpoint. Leave a little slack and fix with a stopper knot around the halyard or sheet 90-122cm [3-4ft] ahead of the winch. (If no help is available finish the stopper knot with a rolling hitch). Lay the broomstick over the stopper and rest it against the cockpit side. Now, with the marlinspike pick up the bight of the stopper and commence turning. In a short while this will have gathered up sufficient slack on the halyard or sheet so that the turns can be thrown off the winch barrel. This done, reload the winch, heave tight and collapse the stopper.

RIDING TURN — Clearing a

A sail jammed hard by its halyard or sheet, resulting from a riding turn on the winch, is potentially dangerous. In confined waters or in a strong or rising wind it must be freed without delay. The method described

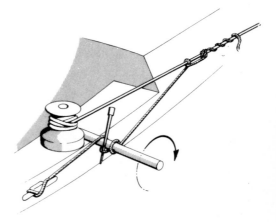

Fig. 91. Clearing a riding turn with a Spanish windlass

On wire halyard it will be first necessary to tape and then clap on one or two bulldog grips which will prevent the stopper from slipping.

RIGGING

Galvanized wire lasts perhaps only two or three seasons before corrosion begins. With care and protection, such as regular dressing in boiled linseed oil and winter stripping, it can be made to last up to 10 years. The great advantage of galvanized wire is that condition can be judged by appearance. As the weather gets into the zinc it darkens and shortly after that surface rusting will appear, especially at the lower end. This is the time to change it.

Stainless steel (SS) is more expensive than galvanized wire but lasts much longer and needs no more than an occasional wipe over with light oil. Its disadvantages are: (a) it is more susceptible to metal fatigue brought on by vibration or drumming, (b) it gives no outward indication of its condition.

The safe criterion is to allot stainless steel rigging a certain lifespan of about 10 years and then renew it. Stainless steel, if brought into contact with zinc (galvanized fittings) will corrode. For the various reasons given many yachtsmen who use SS rigging prefer to have a galvanized wire forestay.

Running rigging The flexible wire used for halyards is made up from a large number of fine wires, sometimes incorporated with rope. The usual constructions are: 6 x 12, 6 x 24 and 6 x 37. The last two are obviously more flexible and incidentally, more prone to stretch. Flexible wire rope can be either SS or galvanized. If SS wire is used the sheaves over which it runs should be increased in size to minimise the onset of metal fatigue. (A diameter ratio of sheave to rope should be a minimum of 12:1.) If this is not possible it is recommended that you use the smallest possible wire (4mm for the average sized boat) and expect to renew this every 2 years. This gives increased flexibility and, since the likelihood of metal fatigue is reduced, a longer lifespan for a smaller initial outlay.

Standing rigging There are several choices including rod rigging which is used almost exclusively by racing craft; the traditional 6 or 7 stranded wire which is rougher on the sails but easier to hand splice, and the more popular 1 x 19 which is stronger and has a much smoother surface. The latter types are obtainable in either SS or galvanized. The 1 x 19 wire in

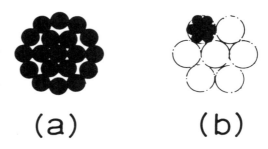

Fig. 92. Non-flexible wire standing rigging: a) 1 x 19; b) 7 x 7

galvanized is better protected because the strands are thicker and can therefore carry a thicker coating of zinc.

Terminals The *Talurit* or *Nicopress* splice which involves machine clamping a thick metal collar around the two parts of wire is suitable for 7 x 7 wire and also for the smaller sizes of 1 x 19 wire on boats up to about 4 tons. Above this the best terminal for the 1 x 19 wire (which unlike the 7 x 7 wire cannot be easily hand-spliced) is the swaged end. Here the wire is inserted into a steel tube which has an eye formed into its end and machine hammered firmly into position. The swaged fitting lasts longer, offers less windage and is the most reliable. An alternative to this is the swageless terminal such as the trade name *Norseman*. This consists of a small cone shaped wedge which when inserted into the end of the wire causes it to expand within a steel sleeve. The advantages of this method are that it can be applied by hand, can be opened for inspection, and removed and used on another wire when the rigging is renewed. (*For suggested rigging wire sizes see Appendix*).

RIGGING FAILURE

Halyard parts *Hoist sail on topping lift, spinnaker halyard, or substitute flag halyard with larger halyard. Reeve off new halyard by stitching ends together or fusing with heat.*

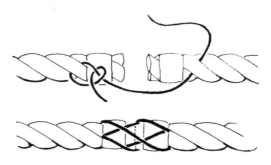

Fig. 94. Reeving off new or larger halyard; ends are stitched together to prevent jamming in block

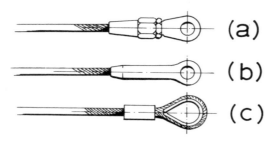

Fig. 93. Terminals: a) Swageless (*Norseman*) b) Swaged end c) Talurit or Nicopress

Forestay parts *The mast is imperilled; immediately let out main sheet and bring boat before the wind. Lower sail (unless jib luff is providing support) and temporarily stay with halyards, topping lift etc. If the break is within reach make an eye in the forestay with bowline, (knots can be tied in wire), or bulldog grips. Set up tight on stemhead with block and tackle, anchor winch, or Spanish windlass. Temporary forestay can be made by using boat's chain cable. Sail on under reduced canvas.*

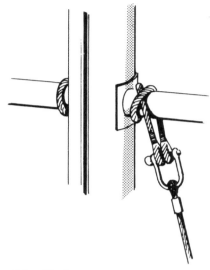

Fig. 96. Broken tang; strop secured to spreaders will carry shroud end and still permit full mainsail to be hoisted

Fig. 95. Damaged wire reinforced with extra length and secured with bulldog grips

Backstay parts *Bring boat into the wind and harden mainsheet. Drop jib and support mast with topping lift, flag halyard, main halyard etc.*

Shroud parts *Go about so that broken shroud is on lee side. Keep boat hard on the wind while halyards are set up in its place.*

Spreader goes *Same immediate drill as for broken shroud. A spinnaker pole or boom will need to be rigged from on deck as an emergency spreader long enough to give requisite angle. (Rig from on deck if the spinnaker pole mast fitting is not strong enough.) The boom is trimmed by guys and secured below the block and tackle onto the chain plates.*

(See also: JURY RIG).

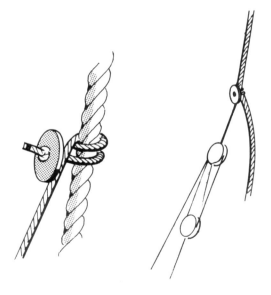

Fig. 97. Winch failure — block and tackle with shivver hitch allows both hands to be used to haul tight sheets and halyards

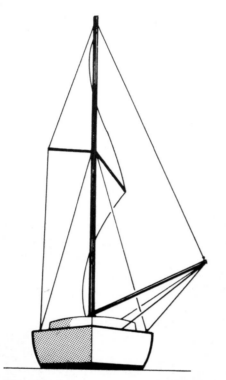

Fig. 98. Broken spreader; spinnaker boom rigged to support mast

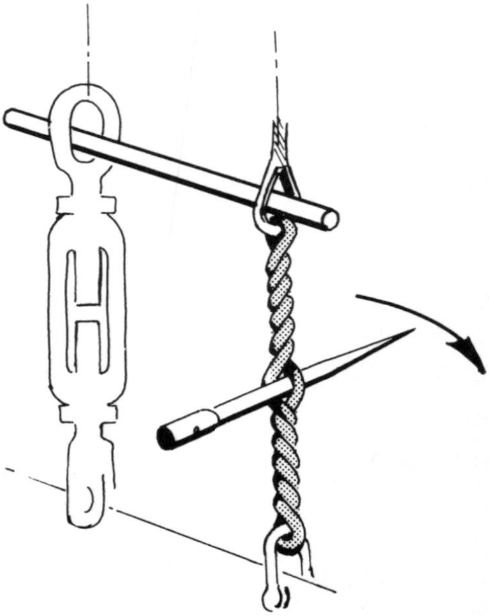

Fig. 99. Broken rigging screw; shroud set up with Spanish windlass

ROPE

Synthetic rope This is stronger, last longer and is altogether much better value than natural fibre rope. There are four main synthetic materials used for ropes: nylon, polyester, Polythene and polypropylene. of the four, nylon is the strongest and, very roughly, comparative strengths might be accorded like this: nylon 10; polyester 8; polypropylene 7; Polythene 6. On the same scale: manilla 5; sisal 4; 6 x 12 wire 20; 6 x 24 wire 30. Synthetic ropes have different qualities. Nylon for example has good stretch properties making it ideal for anchor warps, flag halyards etc. Polyester, on the other hand, has very limited stretch while pre-stretched polyester has almost none at all. This makes it perfect for halyards. Polypropylene floats and is therefore the most suitable rope to use for heaving lines or for any specific job where there is a danger of fouling the propeller. Polythene is hard on the hands but inexpensive. Nowadays, the strength of the rope is related to its diameter but of more concern to the small boat man will be that the rope is large enough to be comfortable when handled. Choose a thicker rope whenever possible.

Construction of synthetic rope

Three-stranded (or hawser laid) The traditional twisted rope normally laid up right-handed. Easy to eyesplice. Disadvantages are that it kinks easily and requires greater care in coiling and handling.

Plaited This consists of either 8 or 16 strands plaited together. The 8-strand have a nobbly surface and are easy to grip. The 16-strand is smoother and provides a better grip when used on a winch. Plaited ropes have lower stretch characteristics, are stronger and will not easily distort.

Braided A very much improved type of plaited rope. Braided ropes are really two ropes in one with an inner core and an

Type	Trade Name	Qualities	Uses
Polyamide or nylon	'Nylon'	Very strong with great elasticity	Anchor warps, mooring warps, sheets, flag and burgee halyards
Polyester	'Terylene' 'Tergal' 'Dacron'	Slightly weaker than nylon, with stretch properties. Good wear resistance	Running gear, halyards, sheets, (Pre-stretched polyesters also available)
Polythene	'Courlene'	Slightly stronger than natural fibre, good stretch, floats in water, relatively cheap, hard and liable to slip	Mooring warps, heaving lines
Polypropylene	'Ulstron'	Slightly weaker than polyester, permanently buoyant, extremely lightweight, economical	General purpose, sheets, mooring warps, lines for lifebelts, heaving lines.

outer sleeve. This increases their resistance to wear, provides for much softer handling, gives a far better grip on the winch, is stronger, free from kinks and with low stretch characteristics. Braided ropes should be coiled in figure of eight loops to prevent permanent twists being incurred.

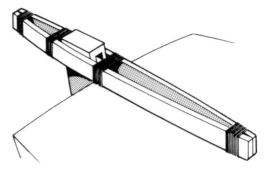

Fig. 100.   Replacement for broken tiller

RUDDER BROKEN

A rudderless boat can be steered slowly in quiet conditions by:

Securing the dinghy alongside and steering with the outboard motor.

Suspending a weight from the boom and dunking this into the water on the desired side to pivot the boat around.

By having a crew member stand on each side with a bucket to lower into the water, whenever a sheer is required.

Towing a partially flooded dinghy (or a lifebuoy or a tyre with a line to each quarter. Steer by working the lines.

Utilising the auxiliary rudder of a self-steering gear but only under reduced sail conditions.

Jury rig If the distance to be covered is large and a better speed has to be maintained, or if the weather is unsettled, then a jury rig rudder will have to be constructed. If it is simply the rudder mechanism which has broken, then it may be possible to rig tiller lines onto the trailing edge of the

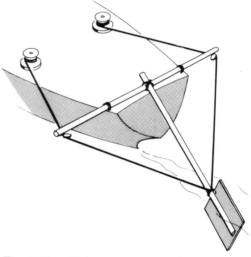

Fig. 101.   Using a sweep. Arrangement will have to be weighted and a topping lift may also have to be used

rudder. These are secured through a hole drilled in the rudder or fixed in position with a 'G' clamp. The tiller lines are taken well forward through blocks on the gunwhales and back to the cockpit winches. If it is not possible to use the existing rudder then a sweep comprising spinnaker pole, door, hatch, floor board etc will have to be rigged. It will almost certainly need to be ballasted and probably supported by a topping lift. For the best leverage the tiller lines controlling the sweep will have to be led as far outboard as possible — ideally through a boom placed across the transom with blocks secured to each end.

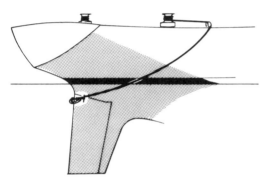

Fig. 102.   Steering with tiller lines led to winches

Using sails A certain amount of trial and error will be required to get the right balance but once this is achieved the sails alone should hold the boat on a steady course. Sails with greatest steering effect are jib, staysail and mizzen (a spare jib set on the backstay and boomed with an oar makes a useful mizzen while a storm jib set up on a spinnaker halyard and tacked down to a mid position on the foredeck can be used as a staysail). The staysail has the most steadying effect on the course and to do this job it is best sheeted to windward. Lee or weather helm, which will be more pronounced if the main is set, must be eliminated. (Reduce

weather helm by reefing mainsail and using large headsail). Steer the boat by playing the jib sheets or trimming the mizzen, probably in conjunction with a sweep.

RULE OF THE ROAD

Under the International Regulations for the Prevention of Collision at Sea (1977) sailing vessels are required to keep out of each other's way as follows:

WITH THE WIND ON DIFFERENT SIDES :—
VESSEL ON STARBOARD TACK HAS
RIGHT OF WAY.

WHEN BOTH HAVE THE WIND ON THE
SAME SIDE :— VESSEL TO LEEWARD
HAS RIGHT OF WAY.

IN CASES OF UNCERTAINTY :-
VESSEL ON PORT TACK MUST
GIVE WAY .

VESSELS FISHING .

.... AND VESSELS THEY
ARE OVERTAKING .

Sailing vessels are also required to keep out of the way of:

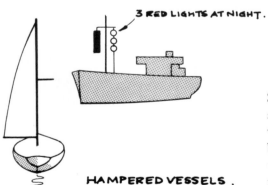

3 RED LIGHTS AT NIGHT.

HAMPERED VESSELS .

Sailing vessels when proceeding under sails and engine are classified as power driven vessels. They must show a black cone signal by day or masthead steaming light by night (tri-colour lantern must *not* be used). They must give way to:

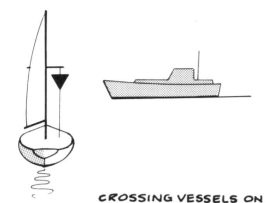

CROSSING VESSELS ON
THE STARBOARD SIDE.

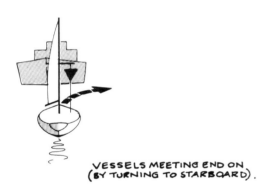

VESSELS MEETING END ON
(BY TURNING TO STARBOARD).

···· AND SAILING VESSELS.

SAIL REPAIR

A damaged sail should be repaired as soon as possible before damage spreads. Apply a few rough stitches or a piece of adhesive tape while the sail is drawing. A sail repair kit should be on board and it should include: a selection of sail needles from size 13 downwards (the higher the number the smaller the needle), some sail cloth samples to match the material and weight of each sail, Terylene sail twine (if natural fibre sail twine is used it must be well rubbed with beeswax), a sewing palm, scissors and adhesive tape.

Round seam This is not recommended for anything but emergency repair while the sail is hoisted. The method draws the cloth together to an extent where the material bunches up and over-stretching is likely and the strain imposed may pull the stitches out. It is however a quick, simple join and one that most people know.

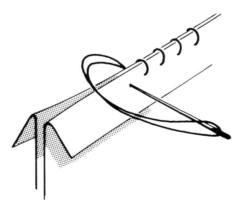

Fig. 103.   Round Seam

Herring-bone stitch This is used for repairing tears and it is far superior than the round seam because the two edges of cloth are held together neatly without distortion. To spread the load, stitches should alternate long and short and should be begun beyond the tear where the material is sound. Use doubled thread and do not pull stitches too tight.

one position more than in another. Start at top right-hand corner and sew the patch on with a flat seam stitch. Draw a pencil line around the edge where the patch will come if this will help to guide stitches. Once the patch has been sewn on turn the sail over and carefully trim the edges of the tear into a neat square or rectangular shape. Mitre-cut the corners and fold the edges under once more, rubbing the creases with the back of a knife. Sew the edges onto the patch with a flat seam stitch.

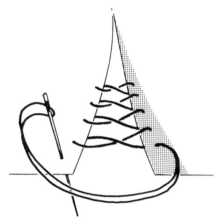

Fig. 104.   Herring bone stitch

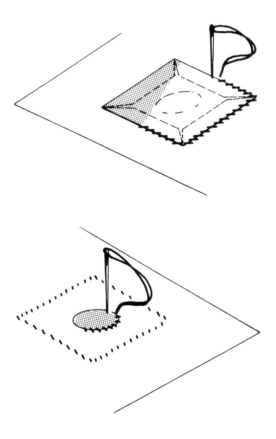

Patching Use sail cloth to match the sail and cut in to a square or rectangular shape large enough to cover the tear. Tuck edges under to produce narrow fold, (these will stay permanent if rubbed with the back of a knife), and mitre-cut corners to prevent excessive build up of cloth. Arrange the patch over the tear so that the threads in the patch run the same way as those in the sail and use pins or sail needles to hold it in position. Make a series of pencil marks around the edge of the patch and onto the sail to act as a guide when sewing. This will ensure that the cloth does not gather up in

Fig. 108.   Applying a patch

Flat seam This is one of the most common stitches in general canvas work and is used for joining two materials together. In sail repair it can be used when a new cloth has to be put into a sail. The edges of each cloth are folded under and a small overlap is made. One side of the seam is stitched to begin with then the work is turned over and the other side is stitched. Apart from neat and regular stitches the main concern is to keep one or other of the cloths from bunching up. This is best done with a sail hook (or safety pin) fixed to the far end of the seam and secured to keep both cloths under equal tension (It is usual to do the work on your lap working from right to left and tucking the completed part under your leg thus keeping the seam stretched tight.) Flat seam stitches should run at an angle of 45 degrees and there is a working rule which says 10 stitches to the length of the needle.

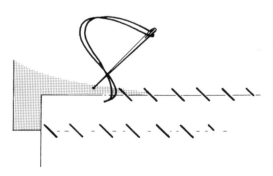

Fig. 106. Flat seam

Machine stitch This is an alternative method of stitching a flat seam and simulates the original stitch made by the sewing machine which is probably zigzag. When repairing a seam this is the easiest method: pick out the loose threads and then stitch into the original holes. Sewing is done in two stages; tack in and out along the seam then turn over, go back, and fill in the gaps.

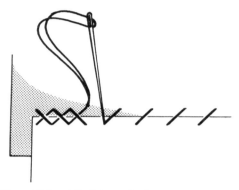

Fig. 107. Machine stitch

Glueing This is a quick and temporary alternative to stitching. It is especially useful where a long seam has to be joined. A good quality contact adhesive is required, but not of the thrixiotropic variety. The method of application is important. Pick out the loose threads and ends and thoroughly clean two surfaces to be joined. This is best done with a nail brush and a small amount of liquid detergent. Clean afterwards with fresh water and rub with a towel to dry. Stretch out the sail, apply adhesive to both surfaces and allow to touch dry — this usually takes about 10 minutes. Then, working from the part of the seam which is undamaged, bring the two surfaces together with light pressure taking care to keep even tension and allowing no wrinkles to form. Once this is complete take a block of wood and a hammer and, choosing a sound base, place the wood on the seam and beat heavily with the hammer. Work along the entire join in this fashion until the two parts are soundly beaten together.

Self adhesive mending tape This is useful for small tears. In emergency, medical sticking plaster can be used.

Eyelets and cringles Few boats will have the correct size eyelets or punches and in most cases if an eyelet pulls out it will have to be replaced with a rope grommet sewn into the sail. The grommet is made from a single strand of rope which is slightly longer than three times the final circumference desired. The grommet is made by laying up the strand in a circle, allowing it to follow

at the sides until the grommet is completely hidden from view. Two lengths of twine may be threaded in the needle together to build up the bulk and give more shape to the eye.

Cringles are the round brass thimbles secured to the edge of the sail with rope and are used to facilitate slab reefing. The rope is made up into four parts from a single strand by passing the strand through the eyelets in the sail and twisting it in the style of a grommet. It is formed, but not completed, before the brass thimble has been placed in position. For a tight fit make the rope cringle smaller than the thimble and use a fid to stretch it. Once the thimble has been placed in position the ends of the rope are knotted and secured.

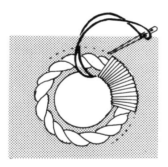

Fig. 108. Sewing in a rope grommet as an eyelet

its natural twist. This will leave two ends which are joined with an overhand knot, halved and tucked back into the lay in the manner of a long splice. Place the grommet over the hole in the sail and pencil around the outside of it. With the pencil line as a guide and using doubled twine sew the grommet onto the canvas passing the needle up through the hole in the centre and down

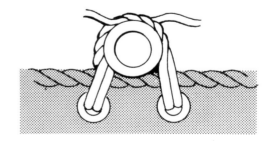

Fig. 109. Working in a cringle

Roping is used for stitching the bolt rope to the sail. It requires a large needle, double thread and preferably a roping palm. Work from left to right stitching beneath each strand. Pinning may be necessary to prevent the sail from spiralling around the rope. Remember it is the rope which bears the strain so aim to get a tight rope and slack sail by bending the work away from you as you sew and sinking the stitches well into the rope.

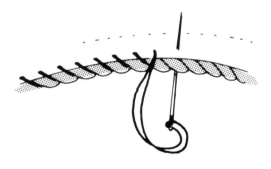

Fig. 110.   Roping

Reefing points Replacement of these will mean following the pattern already adopted. A popular method is to pass the new line through the eyelet, securing it in position by making a 'crows foot', (simply twist the rope against the lay until each strand individually kinks), and stitching this to the sail. Do this on both sides of the sail. New reefing points must be securely whipped with a sail-maker's whipping. This stitches the twine to the rope and thus prevents it from unravelling no matter the amount of flogging.

SEASICKNESS

The important thing is to stay on your feet, stay on deck and fight it. A sufferer feels better lying down but this is illusionary in-as-much as he or she may become bed-ridden for a couple of days and be a nuisance to themselves and everybody. Stay on deck at all costs but make it easy on yourself. Change course (or request a change of course) if it provides a kinder motion and reef the sails if you have to. Find some demanding, responsible job but nothing too exhausting — helming is excellent thereapy. Wear a safety harness and try to keep off the foredeck where your unsteadiness could be hazardous. Similarly, avoid cooking and navigating and, if possible, contact with obnoxious smells, diesel in particular. If you must go below, ensure that the area is well ventilated and free from tobacco smoke. Try to avoid going into fore peak, engine space or toilet. Keep warm and try to keep up the fluid level if you have been vomiting, sweet fruit juice is best, tea should be avoided. If you are able to take food then so much the better, nutritious foods, such as chocolate, apples, oranges, stewed or dried fruit, nuts, raisins, cheese with bread and butter, biscuits etc. Glucose is especially beneficial. There are a number of anti-seasick preparations sold under various brand names. It is worth experimenting beforehand to find the one best suited to your own needs as some of them do have mild side effects. A common side effect is drowsiness although this is almost certainly to be preferred than the dangerous lethargy which seasickness can cause.

Ladies using oral contraceptives are warned

that these must remain in the stomach to be effective.

SHELTER — Making for

The hardest decision for any small boat owner is whether he should ride out a gale or make for shelter? Pressure from the crew, domestic considerations, business schedules — none of these must be allowed to influence his decision. The safety of the vessel is the only criterion no matter how uncomfortable the outcome may threaten to be. Remember that in bad weather a boat needs all the searoom she can get and this should not be jeopardized in a foolhardy strike for the coast. Here are some of the factors which may govern this choice:

What kind of shelter is it — a harbour, or anchorage in the lee of a headland, sandbank or reef?
Can you reach it in time? How long will it take you to get there — at best and at worst?
Has the boat enough fuel to motor sail and still hold some in reserve?
How safe is the shelter provided now and how safe will it be in a probable wind shift?
Might a more distant and less convenient shelter make a better choice?

Are there any shoal waters, tide rips, exposed headlands or otherwise dangerous waters which have to be crossed?
*Can the shelter be entered safely? *Is it on a lee shore? Is there sufficient depth? Can it be easily recognised?*
Are there any entry restrictions or difficulties? At night, is it lit?
Finally, remember the old adage: 'If in doubt — Stay out!'

*A wide river mouth on a lee shore into which a vessel can navigate easily might be rationally considered, but if entry means having to turn the boat to windward then better to forget it. Similarly, dismiss any bar harbours which lay on a lee shore.
See also:* HEAVY WEATHER, BAR HARBOURS, HEAVING TO).

STOPPING OR SLOWING A BOAT IN EMERGENCY

Throw a bucket, drouge, (or even items of deck furniture or gear), on a line over the stern.
Come into the wind.
Turn to stem current.
Turn in tight circles.
Let go anchor.
Keep standby kedge anchor in cockpit. The boat can be brought to a stop by lowering over stern and allowing it to snub over the bottom.

If collision is unavoidable, try to sheer to prevent head on collision. Prepare fender material, mattresses, cushions etc. Keep hands and limbs clear.

*Letting go the main bower anchor while moving quickly through the water is an extreme measure and every attempt should first be made to slow the boat. Unless the run of the cable can be checked by squeezing it with a well protected foot into the bow fairlead the boat may sheer wildly as the cable end is reached. If cable cannot be checked stand well clear of the foredeck.

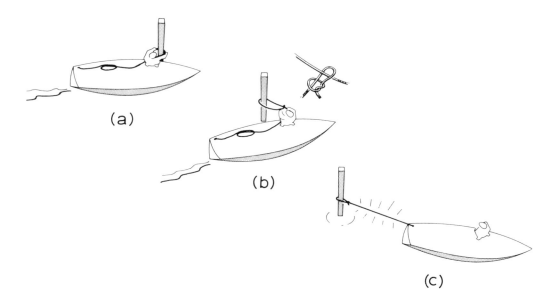

(a)

(b)

(c)

Fig. 111.   Using the mooring pile to arrest boat's movement.
a) Line from aft carried forward and passed around pile.
b) Line made fast quickly with slip knot (overhand knot around standing part).
c) Boat brought up

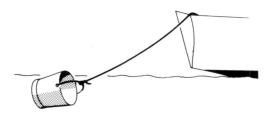

Fig. 112.   Bucket kicked over the stern on a line will slow the boat in an emergency

Fig. 114.   'Panic line': crew jumps ashore from midships with line secured to bow, catches turn around bollard and surges rope to stop vessel

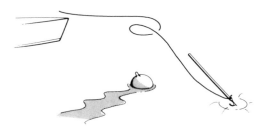

Fig. 113.   Heaving line secured to boathook and thrown uptide of buoy

SWEEPING FOR LOST OBJECTS

Large objects lost in relatively shallow water where the sea bed is smooth can often be located by sweeping. A circular sweep is carried out by anchoring one end of a drag line over the position where the object is thought to lie and motoring the boat in a wide arc. Ideally this should be done at the period of slack water. To ensure that the drag line works efficiently and sweeps over the sea floor, it must be made up of a long length of wire rope or chain secured to the longest length of rope available. Once the object is felt, the boat continues to motor in circles so that sufficient turn may be passed around it. This should hold securely and the object may then either be lifted, grappled for, or at any rate buoyed for recovery by a diver later.

b) Weight of boathook sinks rope around buoy mooring chain, boat is brought up

If two boats can be employed then the chances of location and recovery are improved. The drag line is towed between the boats as they motor up and down with the tide. When the feel of the line indicates an obstruction, the boats should close so that the two ends of the line may be brought together. If a heavy shackle or a chain collar is then passed around the two separate ends and lowered to the bottom on a line, it should succeed in 'tightening the loop' around the object so that it may be lifted by hauling on the two parts of the drag line.

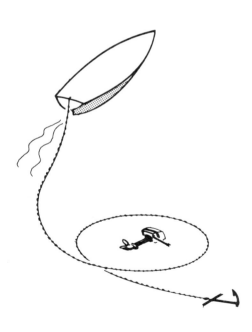

Fig. 115. Sweeping in circles with a single vessel

SURVIVAL

The qualities vital to survive in a liferaft or an open boat are self discipline, cheerfulness and optimism. Organise a daily routine with specific duties for everyone. This will include exercising periods, tidying up, lookout, navigation, supervising rations, fishing, topping up air chambers, repairs, bailing etc. Invent duties if need be. Keep up morale by talking confidently and casually about rescue. Make it a rule not to do or say anthing which deliberately annoys others and see that everyone observes this rule.

Provisions Try to drink and collect as much water as possible before leaving the vessel and then drink no water for the next 24 hours. Thereafter take only ½ litre ½ pint per day unless replenishment is certain. Suck buttons to alleviate thirst but do not drink sea water as this can be fatal. Wet clothing with sea water by day to bring relief, but dry off before sunset as tropical nights can be cold. Do not use sea-water to soften cracked lips. Condensation can be collected from inside liferaft canopy to supplement the water supply. Rain-water should also be collected, lookout should alert crew if rain clouds are seen.

Food is less important than water; a man can survive upwards of 30 days without food, providing he has water. If water is scarce it is important to keep down intake of protein food by proportion. Carbohydrate foods require less water for their digestion and the elimination of waste. The most beneficial food is glucose in sweetmeat form, providing energy and body heat to keep the body fit and preventing dehydration. Sugar and jam are also good. Supplement food rations with sea food but fish or bird flesh should not be eaten unless plenty of fresh water available.

Liferafts These cause seasickness in most people. Take an anti-seasick tablet immediately on entry or the malady will not only drain resolve and strength but will increase body dehydration. It is also important to pass urine within the first two or three hours of boarding the raft otherwise great difficulty will be experienced in doing so later. Keep a good lookout with distress and signalling aids ready to hand. Take great care in protecting rubber tubes from damage by open tins, fish-hooks, open knives, buckles etc. Keep tubes topped up at all times and keep the bottom of the raft dry.

Cold climate Close the canopy, check that there are no CO_2 leaks into the raft, inflate the floor and ensure that it is dry. Cover yourself with spare clothing, blankets etc. Keep moving fingers, toes, feet and hands, clench fists and stretch limbs to help circulation, huddle closely together. When warm, open canopy slightly for ventilation.

Tropics You are frequently in greater danger of being sunburnt aboard a liferaft so keep out of the hot sun as much as possible. Sunburn can disabilitate and exposure to heat will increase dehydration. Unnecessary exercise should be avoided for the same reason. By day, deflate the floor of the raft and slosh sea-water over the canopy to keep the interior cool.

TENDERS

Towing in wave conditions If there is no alternative but to tow, use twin painters and secure from each quarter. This will reduce yawing and is an insurance against losing the dinghy. In a following sea, if the dinghy threatens to over-run the parent vessel, stream warp or improvised drouge (a bucket or a weighted funnel) over the dinghy's stern. Have this coiled in the dinghy in anticipation so that it can be reached and flipped overboard with a boathook.

Bumping alongside at mooring This can best be eliminated if the dinghy is fendered and moored fore and aft alongside. Hanging a bucket over the dinghy's stern so that the tide holds her off may also be tried, but the arrangement has no effect at slack water. Larger boats can rig a spar overside and haul the dinghy out clear on the beam.

TIDES

Tidal rhythm is subject to outside influences; a gale, continuous rain, a dry spell, a river in spate, an abnormally high or low barometer — any of these features can ruin a table of tidy predictions. When making tidal calculations, watch for these influences and if present, expect the tide to be earlier or later, higher or lower, than given.

Assessing tides without tables
It is possible to make a rough guess at the tide from the following information:
Spring tides occur approximately two days after new and full moon; the bigger tide occurs after a new moon.
The time of HW at new and full moon in

any one locality rarely varies more than
½-hour throughout the year.
Very high spring tides are preceeded, and
followed, by very small neaps. The reverse
is also true, that is to say when spring tides
are comparitively small then neap tides
before and after will nearly be as large and
almost the same range.

The time of HW advances on average 50
minutes each day, the actual change varies
between ½ hour and 1¼ hours according
to this rule: 'Big tides, small change. Small
tides, big change.'
The time of low water may be found roughly
by adding or subtracting 6 hours to the time
of HW.

Fig. 116.   Moon cups in right hand — *Waxing*

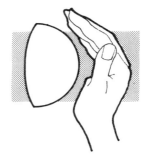

New Moon: Springs — *taking off*

2nd   Quadrant: Neaps   —
moving towards springs

b)   Moon cups in left hand — *Waning*

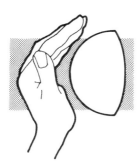

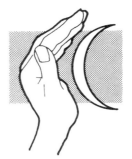

3rd Quadrant: Springs — *taking off*

Last Quadrant: Neaps —
moving towards springs

Calculating height of tide for times outside those given in tables

The *'Twelfth's Rule'* is a rough attempt to mathmetise the unsteady rise and fall of the tide. It divides the *range* into factors of twelve and says that the tide rises (and falls) one/twelfth in first hour, two/twelfths in second hour and so on. It is usually set out thus:

Interval	Rise or fall
1st hour	one/twelfth
2nd hour	two/twelfths
3rd hour	three/twelfths
4th hour	three/twelfths
5th hour	two/twelfths
6th hour	one/twelfth

To use 'Twelfth's Rule' subtract nearest LW from nearest HW to find range. Divide by 12 and appropriate to the required hour.

Example: HW is at 0800 — height given as 6m (18ft) approximately. LW at 1400 hours — height given as 2m 6ft approximately. How high will tide be at 1200 hours?

HW 6m (18ft) — LW 2m (6ft) = RANGE 4m (12ft)

In 1st hour tide falls 1/12th	*of range 4m (12ft)*		=	*0.33m (13in)*
In 2nd hour	*2/12ths*	*,,*	=	*0.66m (26in)*
In 3rd hour	*3/12ths*	*,,*	=	*0.99m (39in)*
In 4th hour	*3/12ths*	*,,*	=	*0.99m (39in)*
		Total	=	*2.97m (9ft 9in)*

Height of tide at 1200 hours is 6m-3m = 3m (18-9ft = 9ft)

Calculating depth of water not given in tables

The 'Twelfth's Rule' will only indicate the *actual* height of the tide around the period of *springs* when LW drops to the level of Chart Datum. At all other times there is far more water than the method suggests. Most boat owners are prepared to accept the inaccuracy because it errs on the side of safety. However, under certain circumstances it can have the reverse effect. Suppose you wished to enter a harbour with a shallow entrance, a bar harbour for example. The 'Twelfth's Rule' might suggest that this was impossible on account of insufficient water. Yet if it were *neaps*, with a LW much higher than that of *springs*, there would almost certainly be plenty of water.

In cases such as this another approximate method of calculation is used:

Find the *day's rise* and double it. (The *day's rise* is the height of the tide for that day, given in the tide tables).

Subtract from this the height of *Mean High Water Springs*. (MHWS will be printed on chart or in Pilot Book).

This gives the approximate *range* of the tide.

The difference between the *range* and the *day's rise* gives the height of LW.

To find the approximate depth of water at any given time apply 'Twelfth's Rule' to '*range*' and add this to height of LW plus depth given on the chart.

TOWING

Passing the towline Do this slowly. Start the engine, lower all sail, prepare towing warp; if sufficient water, steer towards the disabled vessel as shown in Fig. 117. At point A give the skipper your instructions, (you are in charge), and agree on a system of sound or visual signals. At point B you will be head to wind, almost stopped, under control and close enough to pass towline. Directly your stern is clear turn sharply into the direction the other boat is headed C, stop and wait until the line is secured.

Make sure that the slack line does not foul the propeller.

In conditions where it is not possible to get *downwind* of disabled vessel, take up a position upwind and anchor. Float towline down with buoys (fuel cans, fenders) or use heaving line.

Choice of towline It is better for you as the towing vessel to use your own towline because you know its strength and suitability, also it is more convenient when slipping. The use of the disabled vessel's towline

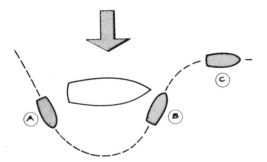

Fig. 117. *Procedure for passing towline:* a) Lower sail, motor close under stern and communicate. b) Hold off to leeward while casualty makes ready, come into wind and stop near to his bow to pass towline. c) Turn sharply in same direction, take the strain slowly

would *not* eliminate an insurance claim, should such arise.

In rough conditions, veer plenty of line, (equivalent to wave length), to absorb heavy shocks. Without a heavy nylon rope, such as an anchor warp, you will probably have to use a combination of mooring lines. In this case instruct the disabled vessel to secure the towline to its anchor and veer this together with sufficient chain to equal a third of the length of the overall tow. The weight of anchor and chain will act as a 'spring' and prevent the line from becoming taut.

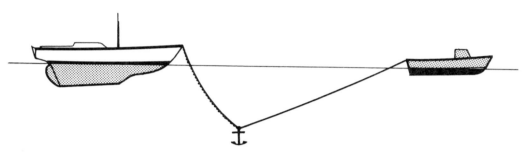

Fig. 118. In sea conditions the use of anchor and cable will act as 'spring' to absorb shocks

Making fast Unless your craft is bigger than the tow make the line fast ahead of the rudder, otherwise steering will be hampered. Jib sheet winches are a good strong point and will make line tending simpler. Make up a bridle if possible so that towline is centred. The foredeck fittings on most boats are insufficiently strong as towage points, except in calm conditions. If the towline is to be made fast here, see that it is 'backed up' either by securing around the deck house or taken to stern cleats or mast (if it is keel stepped). Runabouts and sailing dinghies may be without a foredeck post in which case make fast around the thwart, cabin top, mast etc but also tie down at the bow fairlead or take a turn around the rigging screw to centre the towline. At all costs do not allow towline to chafe.

Towing drill The principle is not to expose the towline to any sudden snatches which could part it, and with every manoeuvre this must be kept in mind. At the commencement of tow bring the disabled vessel to the desired heading with a wide turn; make all course alterations wide. Yawing imparts heavy strains, particularly when the vessel is checked at the end of her yaw. Instruct the tow to steer directly into your wake. In sea conditions, if careful steering does not eliminate yawing the tow should stream warps.

When it becomes necessary to veer more line, surge this carefully; do not let the towline out in a rush — a sudden jar may part it.

Strain in the towline increases with speed, keep this moderate.

Entering confined waters, shorten tow with caution. If the towed vessel is larger she will carry her way further and could possibly run you down. It may be prudent to tow alongside.

Towing under sail on a reach can be done successfully.

Speeds must be compatible. Generally yachts and small craft do not tow well behind big ships and owners should accept well-intended offers from them only as a last resort and then only if ship is prepared to slow down. Big ships' normal speeds are far in excess of the yacht's designed hull speed and there is a grave risk that the yacht will break up. In rough seas there is also a danger that the tow will yaw, become awash and fill up; streaming warps may help.

In rough seas spread oil from towing vessel.

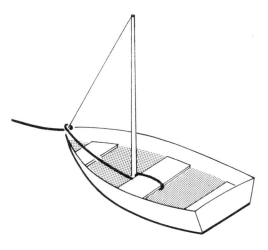

Fig. 120. Sailing dinghy; weight is taken at towline secured to strong position amidships but for good directional pull towline is also secured on stemhead or forestay

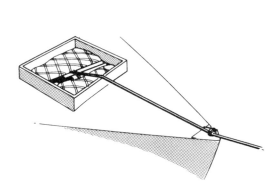

Fig. 119. Small runabouts, cabin boats etc. without strong samson post can be towed with line secured to baulks of timber or oars placed inside the forehatch. Stuff mattresses, bedding etc. in hatch opening. Secure towline on stemhead to prevent broaching

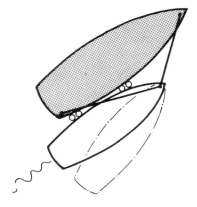

Fig. 121. *Tow alongside* from position well aft to keep good steering control. Use plenty of fenders, weight is taken on spring or 'go-ahead' rope. If possible choose side where tugboat will be able to push disabled vessel into her berth. Use this arrangement in calm waters only

Sailing dinghies Rescue craft will often perform the greatest assistance to a capsized dinghy simply by standing by — downwind with engine stopped and keeping an eye on things. Unless conditions are extreme or the crew inexperienced they should be able to right the boat themselves. If however it is necessary to render assistance, before righting, see that the sails are dropped and secured, that the centre plate is up, self bailers open and all trailing ropes stowed. In reasonable conditions a flooded dinghy is best towed slowly alongside; with self bailers open and boat secured in bow high position she should drain herself. A capsized multi-hull may sometimes be righted by passing a towline abreast the hulls and making fast to the far side hull at a position under water. Take the weight slowly from a beam-on position.

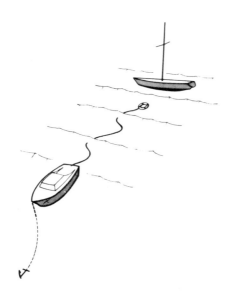

Fig. 122.   In cases where it is not possible to get alongside casualty tow-rope can be floated down or carried across on a dinghy

Towing a vessel off a shore Anchor and float line down, or use a heaving line. A generous scope will be needed to provide both a steady pull and also to keep the tow boat in deep water. Good manoeuvrability is essential; make sure tow line is secured ahead of the rudder. If engine power proves insufficient then anchor and instruct casualty to winch herself off with towline.

TRAFFIC SEPARATION SCHEMES

In general small craft are advised to avoid navigating within Traffic Separation Schemes and wherever possible to keep to the Inshore Zones. (In United Kingdom waters they are permitted to do so under a Government 'M' notice despite the implication contained in the Regulations for the Prevention of Collision at Sea. Rule 10 section d.) Small craft should also avoid crossing a Traffic Separation Scheme but where this is absolutely necessary they are required to cross as nearly as practicable at right angles to the general direction of traffic flow. A small vessel under 20m (65ft) or a sailing vessel must not *impede* the safe navigation of a power-driven vessel following a traffic lane. The word impede is not clearly defined but can be taken to mean that small craft must not anchor, heave to, or stop in a traffic lane. Also such craft should endeavour to maintain a speed of at least 4 knots, motor sailing if necessary. In emergencies a vessel is permitted to stop, heave to or anchor in the 'central reservation' or Separation Zone which lies between the two traffic lanes.

TRIMMING BALLAST

Trimming ballast was once commonly carried aboard every yacht and moved as required for optimum performance. Nowadays with factory built yachts — supposedly weighing the same — the practice has been dropped. But for those who are prepared to carry it the provision of easily movable trimming ballast may still improve performance. It is most convenient to use sand in handy-sized plastic bags. These can easily be moved about and have the particular advantage that the sand shakes down to safely fill whatever awkward corner the bag has been placed in. Moreover it is not expensive to replace should it have to be jettisoned.

The effect of trimming ballast will vary from boat to boat but these are the usual considerations:

Extra ballast, (many factory boats are lightly ballasted), means a stiffer boat, better able to stand up to her sails in strong winds and keep going through short seas and broken water.

If the main ballast is concentrated amidships a jerky motion may be apparent. Trimming ballast placed further forward and aft can reduce this.

A boat which trims by the head is difficult to steer and will probably have pronounced weather helm. Trimming ballast can correct this.

More common is the boat which trims too deeply by the stern as a result of crew together in the cockpit, spacious aft lockers which hold heavy gear, and the siting of the fuel tanks near the stern. Trimming ballast placed forward to bring her to an keel will invariably result in an increase of speed.

Sand ballast can also have other uses; it can be moved aft, loaded into the dinghy or jettisoned in the event of a grounding. It can be used to induce a list should the boat need to lie alongside the quay, or should the waterline need repainting.

A bag of sand can be used as a temporary anchor over rocky ground where loss of the boat's normal anchor is a possibility. It can also be used for *drudging*.

Over ocean depths it can 'anchor' the boat keeping her head to wind and reducing surface drift. When running into shallow water at night, (or in fog), and unsure of soundings, a bag of sand carried under the forefoot will give warning of decreasing depth. Moreover when it strikes the bottom it will automatically bring the boat up and prevent her from grounding.

VOYAGE PLANNING REMINDERS

Once having decided on the voyage to be made, studied the charts, the tide information, the sailing directions, the weather patterns for the past few days and having generally gathered as much knowledge as you can from those familiar with the route and the area, here are a few more customary points to consider:

The approximate courses initially laid on the chart should:
Take the boat progressively from one prominent feature, landmark or navigation mark to the next, and close enough to be within sight or sound of them.

Should not at any point converge with the coast but rather keep parallel with it, or meet it square on.

Avoid obvious dangers such as shoals, tide races and shipping lanes.

Make optimum use of shallow water if heavy shipping is to be encountered.

Take the boat sufficiently clear of headlands should an emergency arise; fog, weather change, tidal streams etc.

Allow sufficient room to manoeuvre in areas where anticipated wind changes could place the boat on a lee shore.

Should wherever possible provide an alternative and take into account areas of shelter and harbours of refuge.

The time of departure may be influenced by:
The need to make the most of a favourable offshore tide.

The height of tide to clear shoals on passage, or the entrance of the place you intend to visit.

The strength and direction of the tidal stream to carry you safely past a prominent headland.

The necessity to arrive at a port, or sail through difficult areas, in daylight if such places are unlit.

Or, alternatively, the need to arrive just before dawn so to be guided by navigation lights — applies to destinations in low lying areas where no prominent features abound.

General Plan to get a compass check for the initial leg even if this means temporarily putting the boat on that heading while passing harbour transits. The length of the first leg will be contingent on many things, not least the crew's ability to stand up to an extended windward beat; if the first leg is very long — then might it be converted to a reach?

Some initial idea of arrival times and alter course positions will have to be worked out, so that the more experienced hands can be on watch when the trickier parts of the passage are expected. Speed of a sailing yacht is unpredictable but 2½ knots is a reasonable allowance. With a fresh crew it may be wise to leave during daylight hours so that they will be accustomed to the boat before nightfall.

While there are obvious advantages in sailing short hops from port to port when outward bound, (especially with small crews and beginners), there is much to be said for trying to reach one's further destination without stopping. The crew will shake down quicker and, if it is a holiday cruise with a time limit, there will then be plenty of time to meander slowly back stopping off

Page 95   WARPING

where you wish without the anxiety and risk of trying to make a deadline. When hopping from port to port try to do so *with* the main stream of flood. This way you can have the benefit of the offshore current and will be able to enter each port on a rising tide, it may also carry you up to the head of rivers and creeks.

WARPING

Warping is manoeuvering a boat using only her ropes. It was the customary way of moving a sailing ship in harbour and in confined spaces and now, with the proliferation of marinas, it is being used aboard yachts more and more.
Entering an inside berth against strong wind or tide;

2 Drop astern.
3 Use second bow line and traverse until boat is immediately astern of her berth.
Boat can now be warped, or motored, directly into her berth.

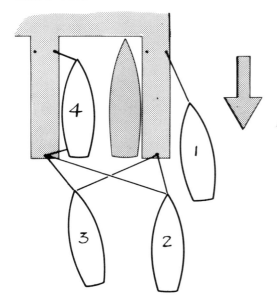

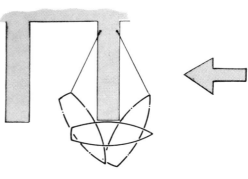

Strong cross current or beam wind;

1 Moor temporarily alongside outer pontoon.

Moor on the end of the pontoon and use bow or stern line to warp into berth.

Strong cross current or beam wind;

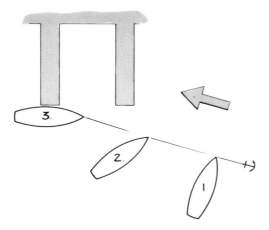

Getting alongside against strong off-shore wind, or cross current sweeping under the pontoon;

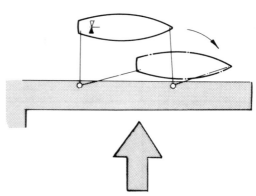

Safest proceedure is to anchor and veer sufficient cable so that boat can drift astern to her berth.

Nose up to pontoon and get bow and stern lines ashore. Make fast. Motor ahead and 'spring' boat into berth where breast lines can be passed ashore.

'Winding ship', or turning her around against the quay;

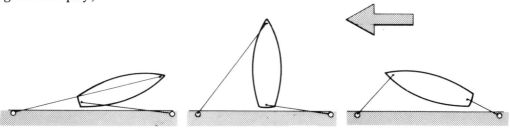

Take advantage of current, in this case from ahead. Take bow line aft outside of everything, stern line forward along quay. Fenders in position aft and breast line let go. Heave on ropes and with help of current boat is turned to face other way.

'Springing off' with currrent;

'Springing off' with engine;

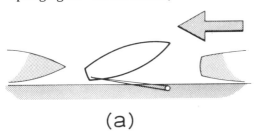

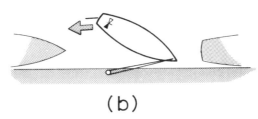

(a)

(b)

Single up to aft backspring. Heave on backspring and allow current to push bow off. When clear motor ahead.

Single up to forward backspring. Go ahead on the engine and steer in towards quay. When stern clear, let go, helm amidships, put engine astern.

Warping often means taking ropes off in a dinghy. Making fast a warp while trying to control the dinghy is difficult. The following show ways of securing a warp quickly and with one hand.

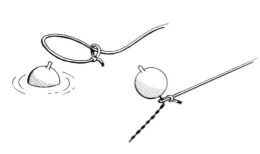

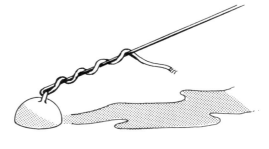

Have a slip knot (running bowline) ready and pass the eye completely over the buoy.

Twist two parts together and hold. This is temporary but will take the weight until a proper knot can be tied.

Cow hitch and toggle (oar loom could be used).

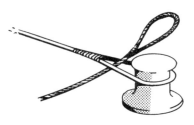

Fig. 123. Eye passed under existing warp allows each to be let go independently

WATERLINE — Marking

Set up the hull so that it is level athwartships and use the remaining indications of waterline (weed, mud, water marks etc), to set level fore and aft. Use wedges to trim hull. Drive stakes into the ground and to these nail planks horizontally as close to the waterline as possible. With an assistant to help, use a chalked line and stretch it horizontally over the planks. Pluck the line so that a chalk mark is left on the hull and repeat as often and where necessary, until the entire waterline has been chalked in. (Without help the chalked line can be made fast to nails driven into the top of the plank). Sight along the chalked line to check it is true and then, using a long wooden batten, pencil in the waterline and scribe into the hull material with a bradawl.

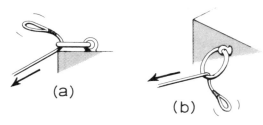

(a)   (b)

Fig. 124. To prevent slip rope jamming when letting go: a) Let go upper end when ringbolt is horizontal. b) Let go from underneath when ringbolt is vertical

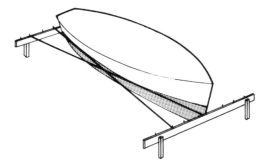

Fig. 125. Marking a waterline

WAVE BEHAVIOUR

A small understanding of wave behaviour is essential for safe cruising and most particularly in coastal waters when conditions are rough.

Banks and shoals Any significant decrease in the depth of water will change the wave shape and pattern. Waves rolling over a submerged bank will slow down and crowd up on each other. They will also steepen and, if the water is sufficiently shallow, they will break. An additional complication is that a bank interrupts the neat ranks of waves causing them to bend and close around it. On the down-wave side of the bank and far into the shadow of it the waves will have been bent to such an extent that they will have turned to meet each other. Indeed there will be waves from three directions creating a confused sea over a very wide area.

In average conditions this can be ignored but in strong winds, particularly when backed by an ocean swell, the danger is real. Moreover, at the point where two converging or opposing waves meet there will occur 'pyramid' waves of more than twice the average height. Although short-lived and isolated, 'pyramid' waves are easily the most dangerous waves to be found.

Reflected waves Waves striking a steep clifff or harbour wall will not expend their energy but rather bounce back and travel out to sea again. They meet the incoming waves as they do so and, momentarily, combine to build up a wave of quite remarkable height. This is called a *reflected* or *standing* wave and is particularly dangerous because of its height, steepness and instability. Under certain conditions waves such as these can be met as much as a mile offshore.

Headlands The inevitable outcrop of rocks or shoaling which occurs off a headland has exactly the same effect on waves as a submerged bank. That is to say they are 'tripped up' as they pass over the shallows, causing them to shorten in length, rise up and finally wheel around to converge upon each other. If one imagines that the point of convergence is precisely the place where the headland stands then it is possible to understand how waves may be said to concentrate their force upon headlands, even to the extent of attacking it on both sides. Bold promontories and headlands should be given a wide berth in bad weather.

All these examples underline the point that in bad weather it is safer to stay in deep water and well offshore. The recommendation to keep clear of banks and shoal waters hardly needs stating although what might not be so well understood is that the phenomena described can take place over banks of a depth not normally considered dangerous by yachtsmen. It is not the actual depth but the dramatic *change* in depth which gives rise to these conditions — not only on the bank but over a wide area on the leeward of it. As a cautionary measure consider the chart depths in bad weather and watch for an increase in wave height or change in character not commensurate with existing wind strength and direction.

WEATHER HELM AND LEE HELM

Weather helm

A small amount of weather helm is desirable. It is a safety factor because on those occasions when she is left to her own devices with the helm unattended the boat will come into the wind and stop, go about, or hopefully finish up with her headsail aback in the hove to position. (This is certainly to be preferred to the lee helm effect when the boat will bear away and almost certainly gybe.) Correct amount of weather helm is important. If the boat's helm is heavy in all but light winds, if she persistently gripes up into the wind or luffs, or becomes uncontrollable in the puffs then obviously the amount of weather helm is excessive and unacceptable.

Elimination of weather helm The usual cause is driving the boat too hard. Reduce heel by easing mainsheet, reefing or changing headsail and weather helm should diminish automatically. If it still remains then the condition is endemic and may be removed by the following methods:

Move weights further aft (see: Trimming Ballast).

Rake mast forward.

Contrive to get main drive area of mainsail further forward.

Prevent mainsail twist by use of lee guy or kicking strap.

Shift mainsheet position further aft.

Reduce mainsail area along the leach and increase working headsail area.

Fit short bowsprit (and adopt cutter rig).

Fit rudder skeg extension.

Lee helm

Some boats are designed to have a small amount of Lee helm in light airs in order to reduce weather helm in stronger winds. If Lee helm persists above force 2-3 it must be considered dangerous and steps taken to eliminate it. Methods you can try include moving weights forward, raking the mast further aft. In general terms make the opposite provisions as those taken to reduce weather helm.

CHECK LISTS

Personal gear

Change of dry clothes.
Extra sweaters.
Oilskins, seaboots, sou'wester, neck towel.
Lifejacket.
Safety harness.
Knife.
Torch.
Toilet gear.
Towel.
Non-slip deck shoes.
Shore-going gear.
Sleeping bag.
Passport.
Money.

Preparing for sea

Provisions, water, fuel, engine oil, galley fuel, matches.
Check batteries, navigation lights.
Test engine.
Check steering gear.
Check bilge pump.
Check saftey equipment.
Hoist radar reflector.
Check sea cocks open and clear, cockpit drains.
Check aloft, ensure all loose gear on deck and below is stowed or secured.
Bottom cleaned of growth.
Up-to-date weather forecast.
Barometer checked.
Charts up-to-date.
Notify friends/relatives/Coastguard of intentions.
Customs clearance.

Routine for getting under way

Note wind current and state of tide.
Plan a course of action and tell crew.
Test run engine.
Bend on sails ready for immediate hoisting.
Check overside for trailing lines, fenders or obstructions.
Single up.
Check for movement of nearby traffic.
Detail crew to places and duties.
Lifejackets where necessary.
Lifebuoy ready on deck.
Let go proceed.

Night passage

Check navigation lights, compass lights and torch.
Hoist radar reflector.
Have flares ready.
Have reefing gear ready.
Visual check aloft.
Check halyards, warps and all loose gear on deck is stowed and secure.
Establish watch system.
Prepare hot drinks or food in vacuum flasks.

FOREIGN GOING (Formalities)

Crew must carry passports; some countries require visas, check with embassies before departing. Ship's Official Registration Certificate must be taken. (For UK vessels this may be substituted with a Certificat d'Identite, obtainable from the Royal Yachting Association.) A crew list with names, addresses, age, nationality, etc, must be made out for each country visited. Insurance cover extension may also be required. National flag must be worn, also 'Q' Flag (I require practique) *when entering* harbour, and courtesy flag of host country during stay.

Customs clearance on departure is not usually necessary unless there are foreign nationals aboard. It is however wise to get clearance especially if new foreign-made equipment is on board (includes crew possessions such as cameras, etc). Some larger yachts are eligible for Duty Free Stores in which case Customs Clearance is necessary on departure so that stores may be placed under seal. Clearing Customs on return is absolutely mandatory and it is the skipper's responsibility to ensure that none of the crew attempt to smuggle (violation may lead to the vessel being impounded). 'Q' Flag must be hoisted on arrival and yachts are expected to use an entry port which has Customs facilities. (In the UK, by special concession, one crew member is permitted to go ashore to telephone or otherwise contact Customs Officers if request signal has not been seen.)

Precautions when re-fuelling

Stop the engine.
Forbid smoking.
Turn off cooker, heaters etc.
Close accommodation — ports, hatches, doors etc.
Make sure you are filling the correct tank.
Keep constant watch on tank level.
Immediately clean up any spilled fuel.
Ventilate thoroughly for five minutes before starting engine.

Entering Harbour

Identify harbour beyond all doubt.
Approach at right angles to shore.
Steer compass course; resist temptation to con the boat by eye.
Take soundings.
Hand log, shorten dinghy painter.
Warm engine.
Hoist courtesy ensign at starboard cross-trees.
Hoist practique flag (at night red light over white).
Clear away anchor, have warps, fenders, heaving line, boathook ready.
Watch harbour signals for permission to enter.
Listen for Harbour Master's berthing instructions.
Tell crew what you are doing.

Leaving the boat

Check all flags are stowed.
Seacocks shut off.
Fuel turned off.
Electrics isolated.
Butane gas shut off.
Ventilators open.
Sails stowed.
Halyards frapped clear of mast.
Steering lashed.
Bilges pumped.
Sufficient scope of anchor warp or mooring warp veered.
No possibility of chafe.
Deck gear stowed.
Personal effects and valuables ashore.
Doors and hatches closed.
List any gear to be repaired or replaced.

ENGINE FAULTS

ENGINE FAULTS (4-stroke petrol engine)

Engine will not start

Starter not turning engine.
Battery discharged.
Battery leads corroded, broken or disconnected.
Faulty starter motor or switch.
Starter drive gear dirty or spring broken.
Starter motor jammed in mesh with flywheel.
Starter turns engine slowly.
Battery partly discharged.
Connections loose or dirty.
Sump oil too thick.
Starter motor brushes worn or dirty.
Starter cranks engine normally.
No petrol reaching carburretor.
Fuel tank empty.
Fuel line air leak or blocked.
Pump defective, or blocked.
Filters blocked.
Tank vent blocked.
Petrol reaching carburretor.
Jets blocked.
Choke device faulty.
Air leak in manifold.
Water in petrol.
Dirt in carburettor.
Mixture too rich caused by use of choke when engine warm.
No spark at plug points.
Plugs oiled up.
Porcelain insulators cracked.
No spark at plug leads.
Rotor arm cracked.
Loose LT leads.
Faulty or damp distributor cap.
Distributor points pitted, dirty or incorrectly adjusted.
Condenser faulty.

Carbon brush not making contact with rotor.
No spark at coil lead.
Coil burnt out.
HT lead loose or broken.
Ignition switch faulty.
Points not opening and closing LT circuit.

Engine starts but does not continue to run

Starting control set incorrectly.
HT lead loose.
Ignition switch defective.
Contact-breaker points dirty.
Fuel line blocked or pump faulty.
Tank vent blocked.
Water in petrol.
Air leak in fuel line.
Carburettor needle valve sticking.
Fuel nearly exhausted.

Engine misfires

Plug leads short-circuiting or mixed up.
Plugs dirty, oiled up, porcelain cracked or gap incorrect.
Loose battery connection.
Faulty or damp distributor cap.
Water in petrol.
Dirt in pipeline, fuel pump or filter.
Carburettor needle valve sticking.
Valve sticking, burnt, broken or with incorrect tappet clearance.
Valve spring broken.
Ignition too far retarded (misfires at high speed).
Ignition too far advanced (misfires or 'pinks' when pulling hard).

Engine runs erratically

Fuel mixture too weak.
Fuel supply faulty.
Carburettor flooding.
Ignition timing incorrect.
Inlet valve not closing properly.

Engine lacks power

Low compression due to faulty cylinder head joint, worn piston rings and cylinders or badly-seating valves.
Incorrect valve clearances.
Carburettor jets partly choked.
Exhaust clogged.
Inlet manifold air leak.
Plugs dirty or gap incorrect.
Dirty or incorrectly adjusted contact-breaker points.
Timing too far retarded.
HT lead short-circuiting.
Faulty distributor cap.

Engine stops when throttle closed

Carburettor slow-running jet blocked.
Slow-running setting screw maladjusted.
Valve sticking, burnt or broken.
Valve spring broken.
Plugs dirty or gap too narrow.
Timing too far advanced.
Inlet manifold leak.

Engine 'knocks'

Timing too far advanced.
Worn or loose bearings or pistons.
Engine needs de-coke.

OUTBOARD MOTOR FAULT-FINDING

Engine will not start

Fuel tank empty.
Tank vent blocked.
Fuel line air leak or blocked.
Pump defective or blocked.
Filters blocked.
Carburettor flooding or dirty.
Incorrect fuel/oil mix.
Insufficient choke.
Faulty, dirty or incorrect spark plugs.
Spark plug leads mixed up.

Engine does not idle

Faulty sparking plugs.
Carburettor needs adjustment.
Incorrect fuel mixture.

Engine lacks power

Carburettor requires adjustment.
Faulty sparking plugs.
Fuel supply or filters partially blocked.
Dirt in fuel.
Exhaust clogged.
Engine overheating.

Engine vibrates excessively

Propeller fouled.
Holding clamps or transom fittings loose.
Bent or broken propeller blade.
Carburettor needs adjustment.

Boat gives poor performance

Propeller fouled.
Drive pin sheared.
Clutch is slipping.

DIESEL ENGINE FAULT FINDING

Engine will not start

See if there is fuel at injection pump, if not then check:
Air in fuel system.
Filter blocked or dirty.
Faulty lift pump.
Fuel tank vent blocked.
Fuel tank empty.
If there is fuel at injection pump — check:
Control rod sticking.
Excess fuel control.
Faulty injectors.
Mechanical checks:
Air cleaner blocked or dirty.
Faulty compression.
Incorrect injection timing.
Faulty air throttle.
"Stop" control jammed open.

Engine starts and then stops

Fuel checks:
Air in fuel system.
Filter blocked or dirty.
Faulty lift pump.
Faulty injectors.
Fuel tank vent blocked.
Mechanical checks:
Control rod sticking.
Faulty governor.
Incorrect injection timing.
Poor compression.

Engine knocks

Fuel checks:
Injector pipe blocked or bent, constricted.
Faulty injectors.
Faulty calibration.
Wrong phasing.

Mechanical checks:
Injector timing early.
Worn bearings.
Worn pistons.
Valve spring broken.

Excessive Exhaust Smoke
(Sign of future trouble)

White smoke — check for:
Air leak in fuel system.
Wrong fuel pump timing.
Fuel injection phase angle wrongly set.
Poor compression.
Black smoke — check for:
Faulty injector.
Excess fuel device jammed.
Maximum 'Stop' control set wrongly.
Fuel injection pump delivery valve faulty.
Fuel injection pump calibration wrongly set.

TWO STROKE FAULT-FINDING

Engine will not start — or starts but then stops

Petrol not switched on.
Too much choke.
Fuel contaminated.
Main jet blocked.
Fuel filter blocked.
Tank vent blocked.
Spark plug dirty or gap too large.
Contact breaker points dirty or in-correctly set.
Condensation or water in magneto.
HT Lead loose or broken.
Oil or water in crankcase.

Engine runs roughly

Dirty fuel.
Water in fuel.
Carburettor fuel filter blocked.
Main jet blocked.
Tank vent blocked.
Spark plug faulty, dirty or gap too large.
HT lead loose or broken.

Engine knocks

Overheating — check water cooling.
Engine needs de-carbonising.
Ignition too far advanced.

Engine will not deliver full power

Carburettor requires adjustment.
Ignition retarded too far.
Spark plug dirty.
Contact breaker gap incorrectly set.
Engine needs de-carbonising.
Exhaust pipe blocked, bent or too small.
Cooling system not functioning.
Propeller fouled.

FIRST AID

The following are hints, they are no substitute either for a concise manual or a thorough course in first aid. In serious cases of illness or injury, medical help may be summoned from passing vessels by the signals V (. . . —) *I require assistance* or W (. — —) *I require medical assistance*. These signals can be made by *any* method of signalling. Alternatively radio can be used and medical advice will be broadcast on request by calling the urgency signal "PAN" on 2182 kHz. If patient is to be taken off by helicopter and a tournequet or drugs have been administered, a note must be attached to the patient giving times and details.

Injuries

In the case of a head injury or one that may not be obvious, *do not move* the injured person. Keep him lying down. Do not encourage the injured person to try to move. If it is absolutely necessary to move the injured, drag the body lengthways on a blanket. *Do not jack-knife*. Support all parts of the body equally so that it is in a straight line.

Chock in bunk with pillows and/or rolled blankets, coats, etc to prevent movement due to motion of vessel.

Do not allow the injured to attempt to sit up.

Get the injured person to a doctor as quickly as possible

Cover the injured but do not apply artificial heat such as hot water bottles, etc. Nothing should be given by the mouth to an unconscious or semi-conscious person. Never give alcohol.

If the injury is obvious, such as a broken arm or leg and if the broken bone is sticking through the skin, if necessary act as for Bleeding. Do not try to push the bone back. Do not try to clean the wound. Cover it with a sterile dressing.

Immobilize fractures to prevent movement. Do not try to set the limb. Improvised splints should be well padded. (Sail battens make excellent splints). Do not tie the splints too tightly so as to stop the circulation of the blood. Body splinting is useful. A broken forearm can be tied across the chest or a broken leg to the sound one.

Look out for shock and keep the patient lying down. Do not give stimulants. (*See:* SHOCK).

Reassure the patient that everything possible is being done to get him to medical aid.

Bleeding (external)

Make the injured lie down to prevent fainting. Press a sterile gauze dressing over the wound, using the whole hand. If no dressing is available, use the cleanest thing available such as a freshly laundered handkerchief or hand towel. If a second dressing is necessary *place it over the first* and so on, continuing pressure.

When bleeding has stopped apply a bandage firmly *over all the dressings*; but not so tightly as to stop circulation. It should be possible to feel the pulse beyond the wound (if you know where to find it).

Do not try to clean the wound but keep it clean.

If the bleeding does not stop it may be necessary to apply arterial pressure, (by tourniquet), but this cannot safely be done unless the operator has training in first aid. *Get the injured person to a doctor as quickly as possible.*

Bleeding (internal)

The layman should suspect internal bleeding if, for instance, the patient has had a very heavy fall. The following symptoms may be apparent; light-headedness, pallor, feeling cold, sweating, increase in pulse and breathing rates. If bleeding is severe, extremities become cold, breathing shallow and gasping, the patient complains of thirst, clamours for air, and his pulse becomes rapid and feeble. He may vomit blood mixed with food or partly digested blood, which looks like coffee grounds.

Reassure the patient, get him to relax, loosen tight clothing, make him comfortable, and explain the importance of not moving. (*See*: SHOCK).

Try to obtain a history of the circumstances, which should accompany the patient ashore. Call medical aid and get the patient to a hospital as quickly as possible.

Burns and scalds generally

With diesel oil replacing petrol as a fuel in yachts, the fire risk is lower. Burns are therefore not so likely as scalds, which are the chief hazard when cooking under way in rough weather. Encourage the cook to take the precaution of wearing oilskin trousers and seaboots and plastic gloves.

Large burns or scalds

If the clothing is on fire quench the flames and cool the tissues with cold water. Tear off smouldering clothes (unless actually sticking to the flesh).

Keep the injured person lying down to minimize shock (see below).

Wash the hands thoroughly before touching the injured.

Cut away clothing from the burn. If the cloth sticks *do not pull it away*; cut carefully round it. Remove rings, bangles, belts, boots, before swelling begins.

When transferring patient cover area with a pad of sterile dressing — or freshly laundered hand towels or sheets. Protect from draughts and cold.

Do not prick blisters.

Do not apply bi-carbonate of soda, burn ointment, oil or petroleum jelly. Nothing should be put on bad burns or scalds except the dressing to keep air from the burn.

Give plenty of fluid.

Get the injured person to a doctor as quickly as possible.

Minor burns or scalds

If the skin is not blistered, cold, clean water can be run over the burn to ease pain. Then apply an antiseptic burn cream, which should always be kept in the galley drawer. Petroleum jelly may also be used but is not as good.

If the skin is blistered, do not apply ointment but cover with sterile dressings as above. Do not try to break the blister.

Unless the burn or scald is small get patient to a doctor.

Sunburn

Sunburn is the same as any other burn. If the skin is reddened, but not blistered, apply calomine lotion freely or antiseptic burn cream.

If the skin is blistered cover with a sterile wet dressing using, for instance, a weak solution of bicarbonate of soda (i.e. 2 tablespoons of soda to a litre 2 pints of water).

Do not use greasy ointments.

Extensive severe sunburning is serious and needs prompt medical attention.

Prevention is best. The skipper should keep an eye on inexperienced members of the crew who do not realise that they are becoming sunburned and who often regard yachting as a fine opportunity for sunbathing.

Illness

Do not confuse with seasickness. An ill person looks ill, is listless, may be in pain, vomits, complains of nausea, may have all these symptons.

Get him to lie down.

Take the temperature (not within 20 minutes of eating or drinking).

If it over 100° F it is wise to get the patient to a doctor.

If patient has a high fever, perhaps vomits and complains of a pain in right lower side of stomach, there is cause for anxiety, particularly if the stomach feels hard and is painful to the touch. Apply a cold compress over the pain and get quickly to a doctor. Give no food and very little to drink.

In any case of illness it does no harm whatsoever to give the patient no food but plenty of fluids unless there are symptoms such as those described in the paragraph above.

If the temperature persists, although not particularly high (i.e. 100°F) there is cause for anxiety. Get patient to a doctor.

Shock

A serious injury including burns and scalds, severe bleeding, recurrent vomiting, and seasickness, may cause shock. Shock can be recognised by the following:

Skin is pale, clammy and cold.

Pulse is rapid, i.e. considerably over 70.

Breathing is shallow, rapid and/or irregular.

Person is apprehensive and restless.

Treatment:

Loosen clothing. Reassure patient.

Keep lying down and make him comfortable.

Do not move unnecessarily.

Keep lightly covered if necessary. Do not *apply heat.*

Do not *give alcohol or any form of stimulant.*

Do not *give water if patient has serious abdominal injuries or if patient complains of nausea.*

Do not *give hot or very cold fluids. If patient is thirsty allow a few sips at a time of water.*

It is important to get him to a hospital as quickly as possible as his life may depend upon immediate blood replacement.

Food poisoning causing diarrhoea and vomiting

This is a common complaint when cruising abroad. It is often accompanied by colicky pains in the abdomen.

First take the patient's temperature. If it is over 100° F get patient to a doctor.

Don't give the patient food; but plenty of fluid, especially after bowel movements.

Relief should be experienced within 12 hours, but if diarrhoea and vomiting persist longer than 24 hours get patient to a doctor. *Do not* give purges or laxatives.

Sudden collapse

Apparently healthy persons may suddenly collapse. It may be a heart attack or a stroke. The former possibility is not confined to the aged or even to the middle aged.

It is vital to keep calm and to stop any signs of panic among the crew.

Make immediately for the nearest port where medical aid is known to be, or likely to be, available.

If the yacht has two-way radio, use the appropriate emergency procedure.

Move the collapsed person as little as possible. Use cushions, pillows or rolled blankets to minimise movement due to the motion of the vessel.

Prop the patient in the most comfortable position for breathing; usually half sitting. Tell him not, on any account, to attempt to move.

Loosen tight clothing, collar, tie, belt, braces, trouser top and suspenders. In the case of a female look out for tight-waisted slacks, a tight bra and especially a tight corset or roll-on.

Make sure the patient gets fresh air and that the cabin is free from engine fumes and stuffiness generally.

If conscious, and if patient asks for it, give a sip or two of water. Stimulants should not be given unless patient is accustomed to drinking a fair amount of alcohol, then only a sip or two of whisky or brandy. *If less than fully conscious it is dangerous to attempt to give anything whatsoever by the mouth.*

In the meantime, assure the patient that everything possible is being done, that he will be all right. Someone should stay beside him. If that is not possible, do not leave him alone for long.

If breathing stops, start mouth-to-mouth resuscitation and external cardiac compression. (Both may have to be continued while moving patient to hospital.)

As soon as possible make a written note of information that will be useful to the doctor. Have it at hand when telephoning doctor on arrival: (i) Time of collapse; (ii) What was patient doing? (iii) Was there a fall? (iv) Loss of balance? (v) Any complaint about not feeling well or about pain beforehand; (vi) Was there obvious pain at the time; if so, where? (vii) When was the last meal? What was it? (viii) Any other relevant information. Does patient say how he feels?

The apparently drowned

Resuscitation of an apparently drowned person should begin without delay. *Seconds are vital.* First aid, in the form of the mouth-to-mouth method of resuscitation, is by far the best. It should begin before, or as, the person is lifted from the water.

The method is simplicity itself:
Lie the casualty on his back.
Pull back the head as far as possible (like a sword swallower).
Pinch the nose to close it.
Take a normal full breath.
With the lips around the casualty's open mouth exhale forcibly. Alternatively, place a hand over his mouth and blow into the nostrils.
This will inflat his lungs (chest).
Allow chest to deflate.

Repeat the process until breathing has restarted (or you are told to discontinue by the casualty or by a doctor). Do not give up even after one hour.

Then turn casualty on his side so that if he is sick he will not choke with the vomit.

Note:

(a) If the chest does not rise, as a rule the throat is blocked by the tongue rather than by extraneous matter.

(b) Do not waste time trying to empty water from the lungs; get on immediately with the artificial respiration.

(c) Air may be blown into the stomach. If very distended, press gently.

A simple technique of cardiac massage that may restart a heart that has ceased to beat can be learned at first aid classes. It is a valuable adjunct to artificial respiration.

The apparently recovered

Some hours after apparent recovery, the resuscitated person my experience breathlessness, coughing and pain due to water, oil or other foreign matter in the lungs. Unless proper treatment is *immediately* available death is almost inevitable.

Every case of drowning, even when there is apparently complete recovery, should therefore be *rushed* to hospital for at least 24 hours' observation. First aid, although effective, is not enough. An emergency may arise, due to water in the lungs, needing expert treatment if the person is to survive.

It is also vitally important to inform the hospital whether the patient had been in fresh or seawater, and to give the time at which the incident happened and a brief but coherent account of the circumstances. He may not be able to speak for himself on arrival.

(*See*: FATIGUE AND SEASICKNESS).

APPENDIX

BUOYANCY

The buoyancy of a drum, can or any closed vessel, (i.e. the weight in Kg lbs it will support), equals the cubic content in gallons multiplied by 10, minus the weight of the vessel. *Safe* buoyancy is usually taken to be 9/10th of actual buoyancy. This is the weight that the drum will support above, if the weight is slung beneath the drum then a greater weight can be carried.

2 gal (10 litres approx.) petrol can provides 20 lbs (9 Kg) buoyancy; 5 gal (22 litres) oil drum provides 40 lbs (18 Kg) buoyancy; 40 gal (180 litres) oil drum provides 350 lbs (159 Kg) buoyancy.

The average man weighs about 7.3 Kg (16 lbs) in sea water.

CHOOSING ROPES

Table 1 — Halyards (Polyester Braidline or pre-stretched polyester three-strand)

Boat Length overall		Mainsail diameter		Jib diameter		Spinnaker diameter	
m	ft	mm	ins	mm	ins	mm	ins
5	16	6	¼	6	¼	6	¼
7	23	8	5/16	8	5/16	8	5/16
10	33	10	13/32	10	13/32	8	5/16
12	39	12	½	12	½	10	13/32
15	49	12	½	12	½	12	½
(and over)							

Table 2 — Sheets (Polyester Braidline or dinghy sheet for smaller sizes)

Boat Length overall		Main or jib diameter		Genoa diameter		Spinnaker diameter	
m	ft	mm	ins	mm	ins	mm	ins
5	16	10	13/32	10	13/32	8	5/16
7	23	10	13/32	10	13/32	10	13/32
10	33	10	13/32	12	½	12	½
12	39	12	½	14	9/16	14	9/16
15	49	12	½	16	5/8	16	5/8

Table 3 — Anchor (Nylon Braidline or eight-strand plaited)

Boat Length overall		Nylon diameter	
m	ft	mm	ins
5	16	12	½
7	23	12	½
10	33	16	5/8
12	39	18	¾
15	49	20	13/16

Table 4 — Mooring Warps (Staple polypropylene or three-strand nylon)

Boat Length overall		Nylon diameter		Polypropylene diameter	
m	ft	mm	ins	mm	ins
5	16	8	5/16	10	13/32
7	23	12	½	14	9/16
10	33	14	9/16	16	5/8
12	39	16	5/8	20	13/16
15	49	18	¾	22	7/8

Note: The radius of the groove in the sheave of the block should always be larger than the rope passing over it. The diameter ratio of sheave to rope should be a min. of 5:1.

ROPE DIAMETER AND CIRCUMFERENCE METRIC AND IMPERIAL EQUIVALENTS

Circumference	Diameter	Circumference	Diameter
in	mm	in	mm
½	4	1½	12
5/8	5	1⅝	13
¾	6	1¾	14
7/8	7	2	16
1	8	2¼	18
1⅛	9	2½	20
1¼	10	2¾	22
1⅜	11	3	24

CONVERSION FACTORS

FEET TO METRES

Feet	Metres	Feet	Metres	Feet	Metres	Feet	Metres
1	0.30	26	7.92	51	15.54	76	23.16
2	0.61	27	8.23	52	15.85	77	23.47
3	0.91	28	8.53	53	16.15	78	23.77
4	1.22	29	8.84	54	16.46	79	24.08
5	1.52	30	9.14	55	16.76	80	24.38
6	1.83	31	9.45	56	17.07	81	24.69
7	2.13	32	9.75	57	17.37	82	24.99
8	2.44	33	10.06	58	17.68	83	25.30
9	2.74	34	10.36	59	17.98	84	25.60
10	3.05	35	10.67	60	18.29	85	25.91
11	3.35	36	10.97	61	18.59	86	26.21
12	3.66	37	11.28	62	18.90	87	26.52
13	3.96	38	11.58	63	19.20	88	26.82
14	4.27	39	11.89	64	19.51	89	27.13
15	4.57	40	12.19	65	19.81	90	27.43
16	4.88	41	12.50	66	20.12	91	27.74
17	5.18	42	12.80	67	20.42	92	28.04
18	5.49	43	13.11	68	20.73	93	28.35
19	5.79	44	13.41	69	21.03	94	28.65
20	6.10	45	13.72	70	21.34	95	28.96
21	6.40	46	14.02	71	21.64	96	29.26
22	6.71	47	14.33	72	21.95	97	29.57
23	7.01	48	14.63	73	22.25	98	29.87
24	7.32	49	14.94	74	22.56	99	30.18
25	7.62	50	15.24	75	22.86	100	30.48

FATHOMS TO METRES

Fathoms	Metres	Fathoms	Metres	Fathoms	Metres	Fathoms	Metres
1	1.83	26	47.55	51	93.27	76	138.99
2	3.66	27	49.38	52	95.10	77	140.82
3	5.49	28	51.21	53	96.93	78	142.65
4	7.32	29	53.04	54	98.76	79	144.48
5	9.14	30	54.86	55	100.58	80	146.30
6	10.97	31	56.69	56	102.41	81	148.13
7	12.80	32	58.52	57	104.24	82	149.96
8	14.63	33	60.35	58	106.07	83	151.79
9	16.46	34	62.18	59	107.90	84	153.62
10	18.29	35	64.00	60	109.73	85	155.45
11	20.12	36	65.84	61	111.56	86	157.28
12	21.95	37	67.67	62	113.39	87	159.11
13	23.77	38	69.49	63	115.21	88	160.93
14	25.60	39	71.32	64	117.04	89	162.76
15	27.43	40	73.15	65	118.87	90	164.59
16	29.26	41	74.98	66	120.70	91	166.42
17	31.09	42	76.81	67	122.53	92	168.25
18	32.92	43	78.64	68	124.36	93	170.08
19	34.75	44	80.47	69	126.19	94	171.91
20	36.58	45	82.30	70	128.02	95	173.74
21	38.40	46	84.12	71	129.85	96	175.57
22	40.23	47	85.95	72	131.67	97	177.39
23	42.06	48	87.78	73	133.50	98	179.22
24	43.89	49	89.61	74	135.33	99	181.05
25	45.72	50	91.44	75	137.16	100	182.89

	To convert	Multiplied by			
Length	Inches to centimetres	2.54		Cu. metres to cu. feet	35.3
	Centimetres to inches	0.39		Cu. feet to gallons	6.25
	Feet to metres	0.305		Gallons to cu. feet	0.16
	Metres to feet	3.281		Cu. feet to litres	28.33
	Fathoms to metres	0.547		Litres to cu. feet	0.035
	Metres to fathoms	1.828	*Capacity*	Pints to litres	0.568
Area	Sq. feet to sq. metres	0.093		Litres to pints	1.76
	Sq. metres to sq. feet	10.76		Gallons to litres	4.546
	Cu. inches to cu. centimetres	16.4		Litres to gallons	0.22
			Weight	Pounds to kilograms	0.454
Volume	Cu. centimetres to cu. inches	0.061		Kilograms to pounds	2.204
	Cu. feet to cu. metres	0.028		Tons to kilograms	1016.0
				Kilograms to tons	0.0009

DISTANCE TO SEA HORIZON

Height in feet	metres	Distance naut. miles	Height in feet	metres	Distance naut. miles
4	1.22	2.3	100	30.48	11.5
10	3.05	3.6	120	36.58	12.6
15	4.58	4.4	140	42.68	13.6
20	6.10	5.1	150	45.72	14.1
30	9.15	6.3	200	60.96	16.25
40	12.20	7.25	250	76.20	18.2
50	15.24	8.1	300	91.44	19.9
60	18.29	8.9	350	106.68	21.5
70	21.34	9.6	400	121.92	23.0
80	24.39	10.3	450	137.16	24.4
90	27.44	10.9	500	152.40	25.7

DISTINGUISHING LETTERS
OF FISHING BOATS

Aberdeen A.

Aberystwith A.B.

Alloa A.A.

Arbroath A.H.

Ardrossan A.D.

Ayr A.R.

Ballantrae B.A.

Banff B.F.

Barnstaple B.E.

Barrow-in-Furness B.W.

Beaumaris B.S.

Belfast B.

Berwick-on-Tweed B.K.

Bideford B.D.

Blyth B.H.

Borrowsto'ness B.O.

Boston, Lincolnshire B.N.

Bridgewater B.R.

Bristol B.L.

Brixham B.M.

Broadford B.R.D.

Campbeltown C.N.

Cardiff C.F.

Cardigan C.A.

Carlisle C.L.

Carnarvon C.O.

Castlebay, Barra C.Y.

Castletown, Isle of Man C.T.

Chester C.H.

Colchester C.K.

Coleraine C.E.

Cork C.

Cowes, Isle of Wight C.S.

Dartmouth D.H.

Douglas, Isle of Man D.O.

Dover D.R.

Drogheda D.A.

Dublin D.

Dumfries D.S.

Dundalk D.K.

Dundee D.E.

Exeter E.

Falmouth F.H.

Faversham F.

Fleetwood F.D.

Folkstone F.E.

Fowey F.Y.

Fraserburgh F.R.

Galway G.

Glasgow G.W.

Gloucester G.R.

Goole G.E.

Grangemouth G.H.

Granton, Edinburgh G.N.

Greenock G.K.

Grimsby G.Y.

Guernsey G.U.

Hartlepool, West H.L.

Harwich H.H.

Hull H.

Inverness I.N.S.

Ipswich I.H.

Irvine I.E.

Jersey J.

Kirkcaldy K.Y.

Kirkwall K.

Lancaster L.R.

Leith L.H.

Lerwick, Shetland L.K.

Limerick L.

Littlehampton L.I.

Liverpool L.L.

Llanelly L.A.

London L.O.

Londonderry L.Y.

Lowestoft L.T.

Lynn, Norfolk L.N.

Maldon, Essex M.N.

Manchester M.

Marvport M.R.

Middlesburgh M.T.
Milford M.H.
Montrose M.E.
Newcastle on Tyne N.E.
Newhaven, Sussex N.N.
Newport, Monmouth N.T.
Newry N.
Oban O.B.
Padstow P.W.
Peel, Isle of Man P.L.
Penzance P.Z.
Perth P.E.H.
Peterhead P.D.
Plymouth P.H.
Poole, Dorset P.E.
Port Glasgow P.G.W.
Portsmouth P.
Preston P.N.
Ramsey, Isle of Man R.Y.
Ramsgate R.
Rochester R.R.
Rothesay R.O.
Runcorn R.N.
Rye, Sussex R.X.
Salcombe S.E.
St. Ives S.S.
Scarborough S.H.
Scilly S.C.
Shields, North S.N.
Shields, South S.S.S.
Shoreham S.M.
Skibbereen S.
Sligo S.O.
Southampton S.U.
Stockton S.T.
Stornoway S.Y.
Stranraer S.R.
Sunderland S.D.
Swansea S.A.
Tarbert, Loch Fyne T.T.
Teignmouth T.H.
Tralee T.

Troon T.N.
Truro T.O.
Ullapool U.L.
Waterford W.
Westport and Newport (Ireland) W.T.
Wexford W.D.
Weymouth W.H.
Whitby W.Y.
Whitehaven W.A.
Wick W.K.
Wigtown W.N.
Wisbech W.I.
Workington W.O.
Yarmouth, Norfolk Y.H.
Youghal Y.

FOG SIGNALS

Lighthouses, lightships, buoys and fog signal stations use various types of sound
apparatus in the same way as they may
adopt different coloured lights, to assist in
identification. The type of equipment is
listed on the chart and the table below
describes the sound.

(Admiralty List of Lights give each station's
individual characteristics.)

Fog signal and chart abbreviations	Sound omitted
Diaphone (Dia.)	Low, powerful note, ends with a grunt.
Siren (Siren)	Medium power high or low note, or combination of both.
Typhon (Ty.)	Similar to ship's siren — of medium pitch.
Reed (Reed)	'High Piping' note of lowerpower (may be hand operated).

Nautophone (Naut) Electrical instrument with similar note to the Reed.

Electrical Fog Horn (E.F. Horn) Powerful medium pitched note.

Explosive (Explos.) Signal explodes in mid air.

Gun (Gun) Explosive signal from acetylene Gun, accompanied by brilliant flash.

Bell (Bell) Pitch according to weight of bell. Maybe Wave actuated (w.a.) in which case strokes will be irregular.

Gong (Gong) As for Bell.

Whistle (Wh) Low power, low note. (The abbreviation MO indicates that the signal sounds one of more Morse Code characters.)

Fog Detector Light

Projects a narrow, horizontal beam of intense blue light which traverses two bearings over a period of between 8 to 10 minutes. The beam remains fixed for a period of about one minute on one of these extreme bearings then repeats the cycle continuously.

GUIDE TO SIZE OF STANDARD RIGGING

A good guide to the size of standing rigging required for a single spreader masthead rig is:

$(0.35 \times \text{Displacement in lbs}) + 1200 \text{ lbs} =$ Minimum Breaking Load. (For ketch rig allow 85 per cent for main mast and 60 per cent for mizzen).

Table of Minimum Breaking Loads for 1 x 19 Stainless Steel Wire

Minimum Breaking Load		Size of S/S 1 x 19 Wire	
lbs	Kgs	Circ (ins)	Dia. (mm)
1590	720	⅜	3
2820	1280	½	4
4410	2000	⅝	5
6350	2880	¾	6
8640	3920	⅞	7
10200	4640	1	8
12900	5870	1⅛	9
16000	7250	1¼	10
21500	9750	1⅜	11
22900	10400	1½	12

HEIGHT OF WAVES

The height of waves generated by winds can be gauged with reasonable accuracy using Stephenson's formula. This takes into account the 'fetch' or distances from shore at which they are formed. The formula gives the most correct solution in gale force winds when the place of formation is not less than 6 miles distance i.e. when the 'fetch' exceeds 6 miles.

Height of waves in feet = 1.5 multiplied by the sq. root of the 'fetch' in nautical miles.

LIQUID MEASURE

1 gal	Fresh Water weighs 10 lb (4.536 litres) = 0.16 cu ft
1 litre	Fresh Water weighs 1 kilo
1 cu foot	Fresh Water = 6¼ gals and weighs 62.39 lbs (28.38 litres) = 0.028 cu metres
1 cu metre	Fresh Water = 1000 kilos, 35.31 cu ft, 220 gals
1 ton	Fresh Water = 36 cu ft, 224 gals, 1000 litres (approx.)
1 gal	Salt Water weighs 10.27 lbs
1 cu foot	Salt Water weighs 64 lbs
1 ton	Salt Water weighs = 35 cu ft or 218.7 gals
1 gal	Petrol weighs 7 lbs (3.175 kg)

1 litre	Petrol weighs 0.7 kg
1 gal	Diesel weighs 8.7 lbs (3.946 kg)
1 litre	Diesel weighs 0.87 kg
1 imperial gal	= 1.20 US gals
1 US gal	= 0.83 imperial gals
1 US gal	= 3.8 litres
1 US gal	= 231.0 cu ins
1 US gal	= 0.133 cu ft
1 US gal	= weighs 8.331 lbs (fresh water)
1 litre	= 0.264 US gals
1 ton (fresh water)	= 268.8 US gals

10 imperial gals are approx. 12 US gals.

MEASURED MILE TABLE

Secs	5 min	6 min	7 min	8 min	9 min	10 min	11 min	12 min	13 min	14 min	15 min
0	12.00	10.00	8.57	7.50	6.67	6.00	5.46	5.00	4.62	4.29	4.00
10	11.61	9.73	8.37	7.35	6.55	5.90	5.37	4.93	4.56	4.24	3.96
20	11.25	9.47	8.18	7.20	6.43	5.81	5.29	4.86	4.50	4.19	3.91
30	10.91	9.23	8.00	7.06	6.32	5.71	5.22	4.80	4.44	4.14	3.87
40	10.59	9.00	7.83	6.92	6.21	5.63	5.14	4.74	4.39	4.10	3.83
50	10.29	8.78	7.66	6.79	6.10	5.54	5.07	4.68	4.34	4.04	3.79

The table can also be used to find speed in conjunction with the *Patent Log*. Note the time taken to travel one mile; then read off the speed from this table.

RECOMMENDED ANCHOR AND CHAIN SIZES

Boat Length overall		Anchor Weight Danforth or COR		Chain diameter		Length	
m	ft	kg	lbs	mm	ins	m	fthms
5	16	7	15	8	5/16	22	12
7	23	10	20	8	5/16	27	15
9	30	12	25—	9	3/8	46	25
12	39	16	35	9	3/8	55	30
15	49	23	45	10	7/16	55	30

It is impossible to be dogmatic about anchor size or chain size and length of cable. It depends on many factors not least the area in which you cruise. Heavy displacement vessels, with deep keel configuration, or vessels with high superstructure should choose heavier weights of anchor than are given here. If the vessel's displacement is known then the following table of anchor weights will provide a better guide.

Displacement		Bower Anchor		Kedge Anchor	
Kg	Tons	Kg	lbs	Kg	lbs
2000	2	10	20	7.5	15
2000-7000	2-7	15	30	7.5	15
7000-9000	7-9	20	40	10	25
9000-12000	9-12	25	50	15	30
12000-15000	12-15	30	60	15-20	35

SALVAGE

Salvage is a reward paid to anyone who saves, or assists in saving a vessel or her cargo from jeopardy or capture. Generally for a salvage claim to succeed, lives or property must have been in immediate peril. (The actual term is: 'difficult and reasonable apprehension'). To qualify for salvage the assistance must have been carried out voluntarily by one or more third parties who were under no legal or other obligation to act. Also for a claim to be paid the services must have been wholly or partly successful, no matter how expensive the operation might have been; hence the salvage term 'no cure, no pay'. The amount of salvage paid will depend on: the value of the craft and her cargo, the imminence and degree of danger and the amount of risk to which the salvor and his vessel were exposed. Since there is often a considerable amount of money involved the salvor has a maritime lien on the property salved which means he has the legal right to hold the property in his possession until the claim is settled.

Salvage claims are met by insurance companies but they must be genuine. If you accept a tow simply because the wind has dropped, or you have to return for an important engagement or you are in danger of missing a tide then you will have to meet any resulting claims yourself.

Wherever possible, insurers prefer that you and the salvor agreed to a salvage fee on the spot. Not only does this save a considerable amount of time but it usually works out cheaper all round than a subsequent claim for salvage.

Salvage claims are calculated on the salvage value of the property so if your boat is under insured then the insurers will only pay a proportionate part of the salvage claim and you will be left to settle the balance.

(In the United Kingdom lifeboatmen of the RNLI are entitled to claim salvage although this right has so far been exercised only in the minority of cases.)